Quilts A to Z

26 Techniques

Every Quilter
Should Know

Quilts
A to Z

26 Techniques Every Quilter Should Know

by Linda Causee

Sterling Publishing Co., Inc.
New York

Produced by:
The Creative Partners™, LLC
Book Design:
Joyce Lerner
Photography:
Wayne Norton
Photo Stylist:
Carol Wilson Mansfield
Technical Editor:
Ann Harnden

Many thanks to the following for their work piecing the quilts:

Kathryn Causee, Ann Harnden, Faith Horsky, Dawn Kallunki, Ada Le Claire, April MacArthur, Wanda MacLachlan, Mary K. Randall, Jolene Sarnowski, Cheryl Squillace and Gisella Wirth.

Special thanks to:
Faith Horsky who quilted the quilts.

The following companies supplied their products for the projects in this book:

Fairfield Processing Corp.:
Cotton Classic Batting

Clover:
Quick Bias used in
The Lighthouse

Bali Fabrics, Inc.:
Batiks by Princess Mirah Design
for *Honolulu Fantasy*

Benartex:
Pastel Bee Happy by Mary Lou
Weidman for *Pastel Links*
Assorted Bali fabrics for
Squares and Patches
Watercolors by Kimiko Ikedo
for *Buckeye Star*

FreeSpirit:
Freckles and Color Dots for
Streaks of Lightning
Color Connectors by Heide
Stoll-Weber for
Petite Sampler
Prism and Etchings for *Starburst*

Northcott Silks, Inc.:
Artisans Holiday Palette by
Ro Gregg for
Christmas in the Cabin
Funny Farm by Tricia Cribbs for
Stripes and Diamonds
Primitives by Laurie Godin for
Primitive Pinwheels
Wild Iris by Ro Gregg for
Drunkard's Path

Library of Congress Cataloging-in-Publication Data
Available

10 9 8 7 6 5 4 3 2 1

Published by Sterling Publishing Co., Inc.
387 Park Avenue South, New York, NY 10016
© 2006 by The Creative Partners™ LLC
Distributed in Canada by Sterling Publishing
C/o Canadian Manda Group, 165 Dufferin Street
Toronto, Ontario, Canada M6K 3H6
Distributed in the United Kingdom by GMC Distribution Services
Castle Place, 166 High Street, Lewes, East Sussex, England BN7 1XU
Distributed in Australia by Capricorn Link (Australia) Pty. Ltd.
P.O. Box 704, Windsor, NSW 2756, Australia

Sterling ISBN-13: 978-1-4027-2318-6
ISBN-10: 1-4027-2318-0

For information about custom editions, special sales, premium and
corporate purchases, please contact Sterling Special Sales
Department at 800-805-5489 or specialsales@sterlingpub.com.

Introduction

Before you learned to read, you first had to learn your ABC's, the fundamentals of language. Once you had learned your ABC's there was no stopping you! Before long you could be reading the encyclopedia.

Nothing can be more basic than that, and the same is true of quilt making. Once you've learned the ABC's, there will be no stopping you! Soon you'll be able to create any type of quilt.

In this book you'll find a project for every letter of the alphabet along with basic techniques to complete a variety of quilts. If you get through the entire alphabet, you'll be well on your way to mastering the art of quilt making.

If you have always wanted to learn a new quilting technique, but didn't know whom to ask, here is your chance. Here are 26 techniques all neatly arranged in alphabetical order. If you've always wanted to learn how to appliqué, check under A for Appliqué. If Hawaiian quilting has grabbed your attention, try H for Hawaiian. How about making a quilt with quarter-square triangles? Look under Q.

In the techniques section, you'll find each technique explained in detail, and to make things even easier, there is a section of patterns for you to use while you practice your new-found quilting expertise.

By the time you've learned the techniques behind all 26 quilts, no one will challenge your mastery!

Contents

Appliqué

Appliqué is merely the process of cutting designs out of one fabric and then placing them onto another larger fabric. But within that simple explanation, quilters have created the most wonderful and beautiful quilts. Because making an appliqué quilt was a much more labor-intensive craft than creating a patchwork quilt, appliqué quilts were often saved for only special occasions, such as weddings. Today, antique appliqué quilts can sell for over $100,000 cach.

Traditionally all appliqué was created by hand, but now many quilters use their sewing machines. This quilt, however, is made by hand, but it employs some modern twists, such as using freezer paper (yes, the kind you buy in the grocery store) for the templates.

See page 136 for Appliqué techniques.

Spring Basket

Approximate Size: 28¹/₂" x 28¹/₂"

Materials

³/₄ yard light background fabric
¹/₄ yard dark green (first border)
1 yard plaid (second border and basket)
scraps yellow, orange, light pink, dark pink, lavender,
    red, black, medium green, dark green
⁷/₈ yard backing fabric
¹/₃ yard binding fabric
Batting
Freezer paper
Black permanent marker or black embroidery floss

Pattern Pieces (pages 156 to 158)

Cutting

Note: *Refer to Hand Appliqué, page 136, to cut and prepare appliqué patterns.*

Appliqué Pieces

1 Basket, plaid
3 Flowers, light pink
3 Flowers, dark pink
2 Flowers, lavender
8 Flower Centers, yellow
2 Large Leaves, dark green
3 Small Leaves Right, medium green
3 Small Leaves Left, medium green
2 Ladybug Wings, red
1 Ladybug Body and Head, black
2 Butterfly Top Wings (right and left), orange
2 Butterfly Bottom Wings (right and left), yellow
2 Butterfly Bodies, black

Finishing

1 square, 22¹/₂" x 22¹/₂", background fabric
4 strips, 2"-wide, dark green (first border)
4 strips, 3"-wide, plaid (second border)
4 strips, 2¹/₂"-wide, binding

Instructions

Note: *Read Hand Appliqué , page 136, before beginning.*

1. Referring to photograph and placement diagram, position and baste Flower, Leaf, Basket and Ladybug appliqués onto background fabric. (**Diagram 1**)

2. Stitch appliqués in place using an invisible stitch. Remove freezer paper.

3. Cut two 2"-wide border strips to 22¹/₂"; sew to sides of appliquéd background. Cut remaining 2"-wide border strips to 25¹/₂"; sew to top and bottom of quilt. Repeat with 3"-wide second border strips. (**Diagram 2**)

4. Referring to Layout and photograph, position butterflies on quilt top; baste or pin in place. Stitch pieces using matching thread; remove freezer paper.

5. Add dots to ladybug using permanent black marker or French Knots (**Diagram 3**). Add antennae to butterflies and ladybug using black permanent marker or Stem Stitch (**Diagram 4**). Add French Knots at tips of antennae.

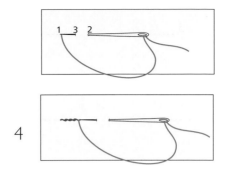

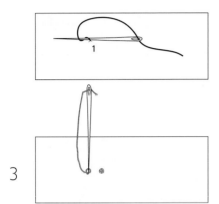

6. Refer to Finishing Your Quilt, pages 152-153, to complete your quilt.

Spring Basket Quilt Layout

Borders

Just as a beautiful frame enhances a picture, so does the perfect border complete a
quilt. A border can be as simple as a piece of fabric taken from the quilt, or it
can be an elaborately pieced design such as the ribbon border in this quilt.

This quilt shows how you can make an entire quilt almost entirely of borders by
starting with a piece of fabric for the center and adding borders around it.
The quilt shown starts with a fabric that was purchased in Juneau, Alaska.
It is reminiscent of the beautiful scenery in our 49th state. Around the central
fabric you will find hidden in the squares of the second border some of the
wildlife that is found in that part of the country.

This quilt begins with a piece of fabric that is 24½" x 20½". If your fabric center is
smaller or larger, you can adjust the borders to accommodate the size of your
fabric. The easiest way is to make the simple borders wider or narrower so
that the next, more complicated border such as the checkerboard or the
ribbon, will fit properly.

If you don't want to make an entire quilt of borders, use any of these borders to
finish a quilt of your choice.

See page 138 for Border techniques.

Memories of Alaska

Approximate Size: 56" x 50"

Materials

3/4 yard scenic fabric (center)
1 3/4 yards dark blue
3/4 yard light blue
1/4 yard purple/blue print 1
1/4 yard purple/blue print 2
1/2 yard medium blue
1/2 yard medium/dark blue
5/8 yard dark blue/purple (flap, binding)
2 1/2 yards backing
Batting

Cutting

24 1/2" x 20 1/2" rectangle, center fabric
2 strips, 1 1/2" x 20 1/2", dark blue (first border)
2 strips, 1 1/2" x 26 1/2", dark blue (first border)
4 strips, 2 1/2"-wide, light blue (second border)
2 strips, 2 1/2"-wide, purple/blue print 1 (second border)
2 strips, 2 1/2"-wide, purple/blue print 2 (second border)
4 strips, 1 1/2"-wide, dark blue/purple (flap)
2 strips, 4 1/2" x 30 1/2", dark blue (third border)
2 strips, 3 1/2" x 38 1/2", dark blue (third border)
15 squares, 3 7/8", medium dark blue (fourth border)
14 squares, 3 7/8", medium blue (fourth border)
2 squares, 3 7/8", light blue (fourth border)
7 squares, 4 1/4", medium dark blue (fourth border)
7 squares, 4 1/4", medium blue (fourth border)
13 squares, 4 1/4", light blue (fourth border)
6 strips, 4 1/2"-wide, dark blue (fifth border)
6 strips, 2 1/2"-wide, binding

Instructions

1. Sew 1 1/2" x 20 1/2" dark blue strips to sides of center fabric; press seams toward border strips. Sew 1 1/2" x 26 1/2" dark blue strips to top and bottom of center fabric; press seams toward border strips. (**Diagram 1**)

2. For second border, sew 2 1/2" light blue strip to 2 1/2" purple/blue print 1; press seam toward darker fabric. Repeat for remaining light blue strips and purple/blue print 1 and purple/blue print 2 for a total of four strip sets. (**Diagram 2**)

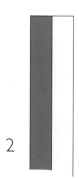

3. Cut strip sets at 2 1/2" intervals for a total of 56 pairs of squares. (**Diagram 3**)

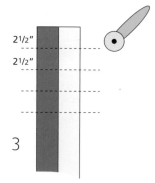

4. Sew eleven pairs of squares in checkerboard fashion; repeat. Sew to sides of quilt. (**Diagram 4**)

6. Sew 17 pairs of squares in checkerboard fashion; repeat. Sew to top and bottom of quilt. (**Diagram 5**)

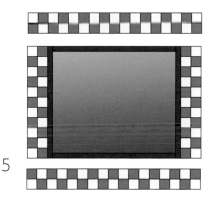

7. For side flaps, cut two 1¹/₂" purple/blue print strips 30¹/₂" long. Fold strips in half lengthwise with wrong sides together. Place along sides of quilt with raw edges even; pin in place. (**Diagram 6**)

8. For third border, place 4¹/₂" x 30¹/₂" dark blue strip right side down on top of flap along side of quilt; sew in place. Repeat on other side. Press seams toward checkerboard border. (**Diagram 7**) **Note**: *Pressing toward checkerboard border is important in order for flap to lie correctly.*

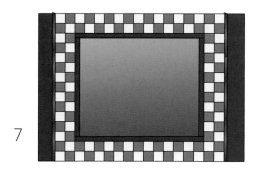

9. For top and bottom flaps, cut two 1¹/₂" purple/blue print strips 38¹/₂" long. Fold strips in half lengthwise with wrong sides together. Place along top and bottom of quilt with raw edges even; pin in place. (**Diagram 8**)

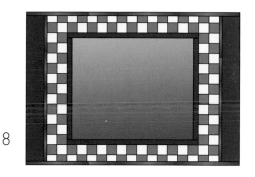

10. Place 3¹/₂" x 38¹/₂" dark blue strip right side down on top of flap along top edge of quilt; sew in place. Repeat on bottom edge. Press seams toward checkerboard border. (**Diagram 9**)

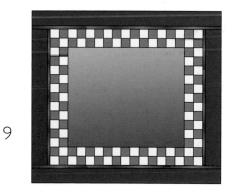

11. For fourth border, cut the 3⁷/₈" dark blue, medium blue and light blue squares in half diagonally. (**Diagram 10**)

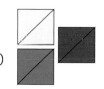

12. Cut the 4¹/₄" dark blue, medium blue and light blue squares in quarters diagonally. (**Diagram 11**)

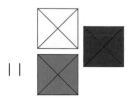

13. Sew small medium blue and light blue triangles together along a short edge. Sew to a large dark blue triangle. (**Diagram 12**) Make 12 more pieced squares.

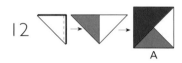

14. Repeat step 13 except switch placement of the small light blue and medium blue triangles. (**Diagram 13**)

15. Sew small dark blue and light blue triangles together along a short edge. Sew to a large medium blue triangle. (**Diagram 14**) Make 12 more pieced squares.

16. Repeat step 13 except switch placement of the small light blue and dark blue triangles. (**Diagram 15**)

17. Sew a large light blue triangle to large dark blue triangle; repeat three more times. (**Diagram 16**)

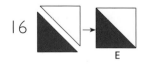

18. For each side border, sew 12 pieced squares together, noting positions. (**Diagram 17**) Sew to sides of quilt.

19. For top and bottom borders, sew 14 pieced squares together, noting positions. Sew corner squares to each end of each border strip. Sew to top and bottom of quilt. (**Diagram 18**)

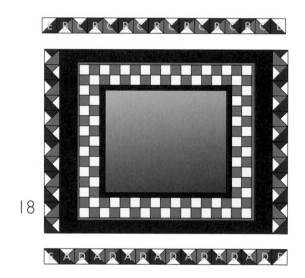

20. Refer to Mitered Borders, pages 138-139, to add 4¹/₂"-wide dark blue fifth border.

21. Refer to Finishing Your Quilt, pages 152-153, to complete your quilt.

Memories of Alaska Quilt Layout

Crazy Quilt

Crazy quilts were probably never intended to provide warmth; rather they served to show the needlework skills of the maker and usually appeared as throws in the parlor rather than covers for beds. Especially popular during the Victorian era, crazy quilts were often made of velvets and silks and embellished with laces, trims, buttons, charms and exquisite hand embroidery.

To the Victorians, the word "crazy" connoted something broken or splintered, rather than insane. Even today the dictionary defines a crazy quilt as a "hodgepodge pieced together without design." The words "crazy quilt" have passed into current usage to describe something that has no readily discernable pattern such as "a crazy quilt of laws."

Traditionally a crazy quilt is built on a foundation of muslin on which assorted shapes of fabric are sewn in a random pattern. This technique of piecing on a foundation has seen new interest as many quilters have adopted this technique to making all kinds of quilts.

See page 140 for Foundation Piecing techniques.

Twisted Paths

Approximate Size: 35^{1}/$_{2}$" x 35^{1}/$_{2}$"

Materials

Assorted scraps of fabrics
1^{1}/$_{4}$ yards black
1 yard muslin (foundation)
1^{1}/$_{4}$ yards backing
^{1}/$_{3}$ yard binding
Batting (optional)
Assorted embellishments and trims

Cutting

4 strips, 1^{3}/$_{4}$" x 7^{1}/$_{2}$", black (sashing)
2 strips, 1^{3}/$_{4}$" x 14^{1}/$_{2}$", black (sashing)
2 strips, 1^{3}/$_{4}$" x 31", black (sashing)
2 strips, 3" x 31", black (border)
2 strips, 3" x 36", black (border)
4 strips, 2^{1}/$_{2}$"-wide, black (binding)

Instructions

BLOCKS
Note: *Refer to Foundation Piecing, pages 140 to 143, to make foundation-pieced blocks.*

1. Make 16 Crazy quilt blocks. Be sure to use muslin as your foundation. Muslin will stabilize the blocks when adding embellishments later. (**Diagram 1**)

I

FINISHING
1. Sew all but four blocks together in pairs. (**Diagram 2**)

2

2. Sew two pairs together for center of quilt. (**Diagram 3**)

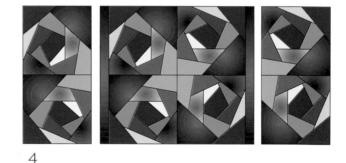

3

3. Sew 1^{3}/$_{4}$" x 14^{1}/$_{2}$" black strip to opposite sides of quilt center; sew a pair of blocks to border strips. (**Diagram 4**)

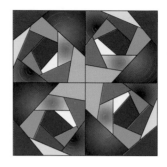

4

4. Sew a 1^{3}/$_{4}$" x 31" black strip to top and bottom of center portion of quilt. (**Diagram 5**)

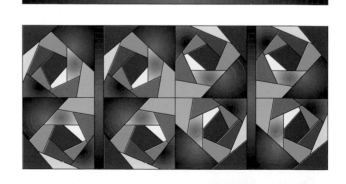

5

5. Sew a 1³/₄" x 7¹/₂" black strip on opposite sides of remaining two pairs of blocks; sew a block to each end. (**Diagram 6**)

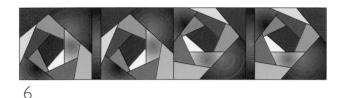

6

6. Sew strips made in step 5 to top and bottom of quilt. (**Diagram 7**)

7. Sew 3" x 31" black strips to sides of quilt. Sew 3" x 36" black strips to top and bottom of quilt.

8. Refer to Finishing Your Quilt, pages 152-153, to complete your quilt.

9. Embroider and add trims as desired. The Blanket Stitch, Cross Stitch and French Knot were used. (**Diagram 8**)

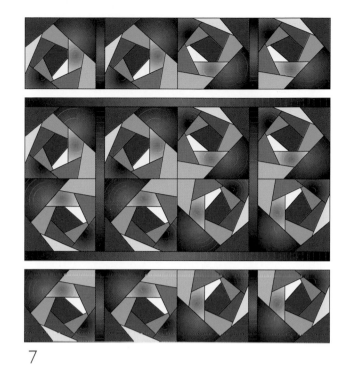

7

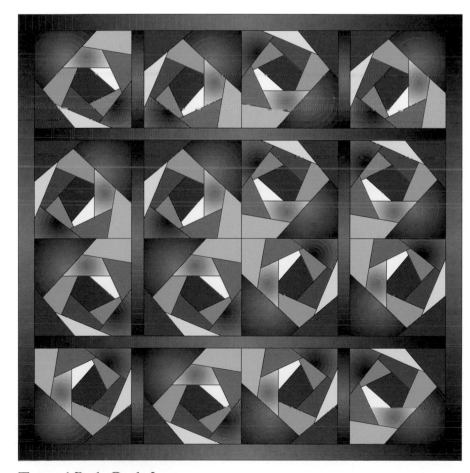

Twisted Path Quilt Layout

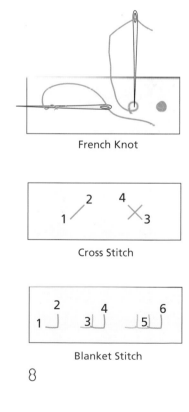

French Knot

Cross Stitch

Blanket Stitch

8

Diagonal Set

Once a block is completed, it must be placed or "set" into the quilt. Diagonal set quilts make use of blocks that are placed on point or diagonally. They are usually more interesting visually than a quilt where the blocks are set in rows, called a "straight set" quilt.

Diagonal set quilts are a little more complex to make because you have to fill in the sides with setting triangles and corners with corner triangles to complete the quilt top, but the results are striking.

See page 147 for Cutting Triangles techniques and page 148 for Stitch and Flip techniques.

Quackers

Approximate Size: 61" x 61"

Materials

1⁵⁄₈ yards novelty print
¹⁄₂ yard light yellow
³⁄₄ yard medium yellow
⁷⁄₈ yard dark yellow
³⁄₈ yard pink
⁵⁄₈ yard dark turquoise
¹⁄₂ yard pink (first border)
1¹⁄₄ yards aqua (second border and binding)
3 yards backing
Batting

Cutting

Blocks

13 squares, 6¹⁄₂", novelty print
3 strips, 2"-wide, light yellow
6 strips, 2"-wide, medium yellow
9 strips, 2"-wide, dark yellow
52 squares, 3¹⁄₂" x 3¹⁄₂", dark turquoise
52 squares, 2" x 2", dark yellow
72 squares, 2" x 2", medium yellow
32 squares, 2" x 2", light yellow
52 squares, 2" x 2", pink

Finishing

2 squares, 20" x 20", novelty print (setting triangles)
2 squares, 12" x 12", novelty print (corner triangles)
6 strips, 2¹⁄₂"-wide, pink (first border)
7 strips, 3¹⁄₂"-wide, aqua (second border)
7 strips, 2¹⁄₂"-wide, binding

Instructions

BLOCK A

1. For Sub-unit A, use the Stitch and Flip method (see page 148) to sew two 2" medium yellow, one 2" pink and one 2" dark yellow square to a 3¹⁄₂" dark turquoise square. Make a total of 36 Sub-unit A.

Place a 2" dark yellow square right sides together with a 3¹⁄₂" dark turquoise square. Sew diagonally from corner to corner of dark yellow square. Trim ¹⁄₄" from stitching then flip resulting triangle over; press. (**Diagram 1**)

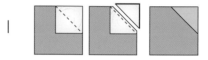

Repeat for pink square and two medium yellow squares. (**Diagram 2**) Note placement of pink and medium yellow squares.

Sub-unit A

2. Sew a 2" dark yellow strip to a 2" medium yellow strip. Repeat for five more pairs of strips. Press seam toward dark yellow strip. Cut strips at 6¹⁄₂" intervals for a total of 36 pairs of strips, 3¹⁄₂" x 6¹⁄₂". (**Diagram 3**)

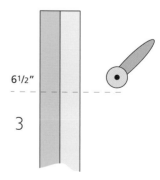

6¹⁄₂"

3

3. Sew a strip pair to opposite sides of a 6$\frac{1}{2}$" novelty print square. Be sure the dark yellow strip is next to the novelty print square. Press seams toward square. (**Diagram 4**)

4

4. Sew a sub-unit A to opposite sides of a strip pair. Be sure that the dark yellow triangles are next to the dark yellow strip and medium yellow triangles are next to medium yellow strip. Repeat. (**Diagram 5**)

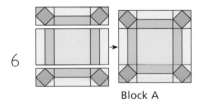

5

5. Sew strips just made to remaining sides of novelty print square to complete Block A. (**Diagram 6**) Make nine block A.

6

Block A

BLOCK B

1. For Sub-unit B, use the Stitch and Flip method to sew two 2" light yellow, one 2" pink and one 2" dark yellow square to a 3$\frac{1}{2}$" dark turquoise square. Make a total of 36 Sub-unit B. (**Diagram 7**)

7

2. Sew a 2" dark yellow strip to a 2" light yellow strip. Repeat for two more pairs of strips. Press seam toward dark yellow strip. Cut strips at 6$\frac{1}{2}$" intervals for a total of 16 pairs of strips, 3$\frac{1}{2}$" x 6$\frac{1}{2}$". (**Diagram 8**)

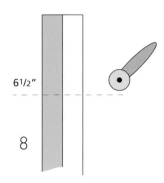

6$\frac{1}{2}$"

8

3. Sew a strip pair to opposite sides of a 6$\frac{1}{2}$" novelty print square. Be sure the dark yellow strip is next to the novelty print square. Press seams toward square. (**Diagram 9**)

9

4. Sew a sub-unit B to opposite sides of a strip pair. Be sure that the dark yellow triangles are next to the dark yellow strip and light yellow triangles are next to light yellow strip. Repeat. (**Diagram 10**)

10

5. Sew strips just made to remaining sides of novelty print square to complete Block B. (**Diagram 11**) Make four Block B.

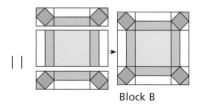

11

Block B

FINISHING THE QUILT

1. Cut the two 20" novelty print squares diagonally in quarters for a total of eight setting triangles. (**Diagram 12**)

12

2. Cut the two 12" novelty print squares diagonally in half for a total of four corner triangles. (**Diagram 13**)

13

3. Place blocks in diagonal rows with setting triangles at the ends of each row. (**Diagram 14**) Note the placement of Blocks A and B.

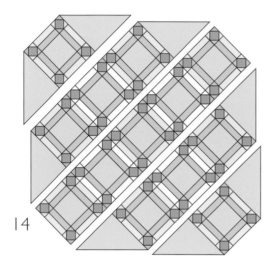

14

4. Sew blocks and triangles together in rows, then sew rows together.

5. Sew corner triangles to each corner. (**Diagram 15**) Press quilt top being careful not to stretch out of shape.

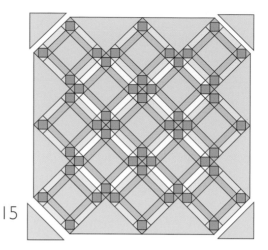

15

6. Measure quilt top lengthwise. Sew and cut 2^1/$_2$"-wide pink strips to that length; repeat. Sew to sides of quilt. Measure quilt top crosswise. Sew and cut 2^1/$_2$"-wide pink strips to that length; repeat. Sew to top and bottom of quilt.

7. Repeat step 6 for second border using 3^1/$_2$"-wide aqua strips.

8. Refer to Finishing Your Quilt, pages 152-153.

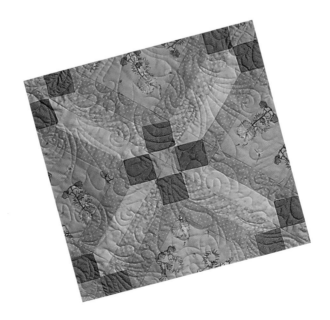

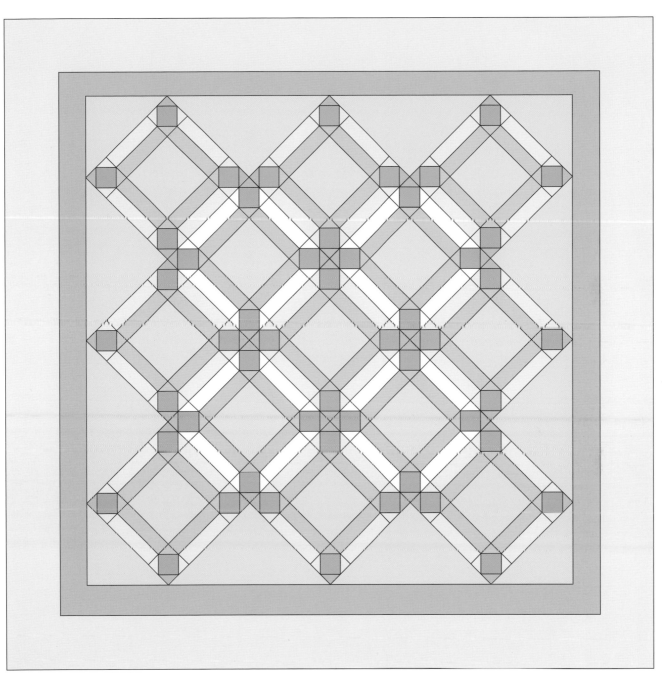

Quackers Quilt Layout

Embroidery

While embroidered quilt blocks have enjoyed popularity among quiltmakers for
years, by far the most popular kind of embroidered quilt was the Redwork
Quilt. Dating back to the late 19th century, Redwork was worked mainly with
a simple stem stitch and Turkey red thread on muslin. The designs were
simple outlines and were mostly intended for children. Because it would be
necessary for a Redwork quilt to survive many washings, it was worked with
embroidery floss developed in the area around Turkey in the 17th century
that remained colorfast. The process to make the floss was very involved and
expensive, but the thread never bled—almost the opposite of red thread
today. The actual process for making this dye was never revealed, and it took
over 100 years for other countries to try to finally duplicate it.

During the early part of the 20th century, Redwork designs were sold preprinted on
muslin squares, called "penny squares" since they sold for a penny each. Many
old quilts from this era, such as the one shown here, contained the same
blocks. The patterns were quite simple; the design themes included animals,
flowers, toys, people and children. The blocks were embroidered and then
sewn together. Sometimes a feather, herringbone or cross-stitch was used to
cover the seams between the blocks.

See page 145 for Redwork Embroidery techniques.

Redwork Coverlet

Approximate Size: 31" x 48" (without ruffle)

The antique coverlet shown here dates as far back 1880s. This was determined by the Baseball player motif in the lower left of the coverlet.

Materials

4 yards muslin (includes backing)
Red embroidery floss
Removable fabric marker or thin lead pencil
Thin batting

Patterns *(pages 160 to 177)*

Cutting

18 squares, 10½" x 10½", muslin
4"-wide strips, muslin (border)
5 strips, 7¼"-wide, muslin (ruffle) 180" long

Instructions

BLOCKS

1. Trace each pattern centered on a muslin square. Use a fine lead pencil or a removable fabric marker.

2. Embroider along marked lines using a Stem Stitch. (**Diagram 1**)

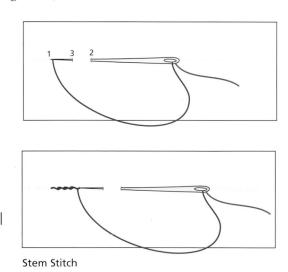

I

Stem Stitch

3. Trim blocks to 8½" square.

FINISHING

1. Place blocks in six rows of three blocks. Sew together in rows then sew rows together. (**Diagram 2**)

2. Measure your coverlet lengthwise. Sew and cut border strips to that length then sew to sides of coverlet. (**Diagram 3**)

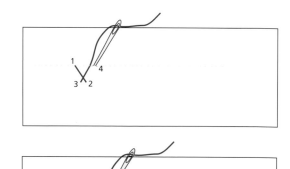

2   3

3. Cover seams between and along blocks and borders with the Herringbone Stitch. (**Diagram 4**)

4

Herringbone Stitch

4. For ruffle, sew strips together end to end to make a long strip 180". Fold one long end under ¼"; press. Fold another ¾" and press. Stitch near first fold. (**Diagram 5**)

5. Fold under short ends of ruffle strip ¼", then another ¾". Stitch near first fold.

6. Make ¼" to ½" pleats every 2" to 3" along raw edge of ruffle strip. (**Diagram 6**)

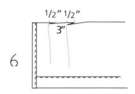

7. Pin pleated edge of ruffle right sides together with the sides and bottom of the coverlet. Make more pleats if needed. (**Diagram 7**) Baste ruffle to quilt top.

8. Cut backing and batting to equal coverlet size; place coverlet and backing right sides together with batting on the bottom. Ruffle will be between coverlet top and backing. Sew together along the three sides with ruffle. (**Diagram 8**)

9. Turn coverlet right side out. Fold top edges toward inside; sew close to folded edge to complete coverlet.

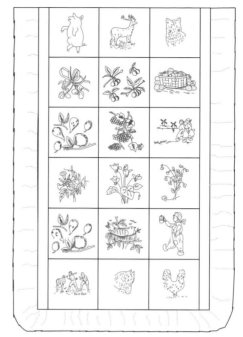

Redwork Coverlet Layout

Foundation Piecing

If using templates—the traditional method of quiltmaking—doesn't appeal to you because you don't enjoy the process of measuring, cutting bits of fabric, and then sewing everything back together, try Foundation Piecing!

In this process the patchwork pieces are sewn onto a foundation of either paper or cloth. Every piece—even the smallest—meets every other piece precisely and accurately with a minimum of stress on the part of the quilter. It's like "paint by numbers" for quilt making—just as easy and just as much fun!

Once you start foundation piecing, you may never return to the traditional templates. In fact, you might soon look at every quilt as a possible foundation pattern

See Page 140 for Foundation Piecing techniques.

Carpenter's Wheels

Approximate Size: 54" x 68"

Materials

1 1/2 yards burgundy floral
1/2 yard light pink
1 1/2 yards turquoise floral
1/2 yard light blue
1 yard gold
2 yards light beige
1/2 yard gold (first border)
7/8 yard burgundy floral (second border)
5/8 yard binding
3 1/2 yards backing
Batting

Cutting

Note: *You do not need to cut exact pieces for foundation piecing. It would be helpful to cut fabric into strips large enough to cover spaces (see Cutting the Fabric, page 140).*

Finishing

6 strips, 2 1/2"-wide, gold (first border)
6 strips, 4 1/2"-wide, burgundy floral (second border)
7 strips, 2 1/2"-wide, binding

Instructions

Note: *Read Foundation Piecing instructions pages 140-143, before beginning.*

1. Referring to How to Make a Foundation, make 24 Block A foundations using pattern on page 178 and 24 Block B foundations using pattern on page 179. (**Diagram 1**) **Note:** *Patterns for Block A and B are the same except for color placement.*

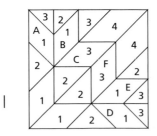

2. Cut foundations apart in sections. (**Diagram 2**)

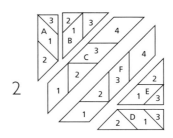

3. Starting with Block A, sew each section. (**Diagram 3**)

4. Sew sections together to make a quarter of the block. (**Diagram 4**) Make four quarters for each block.

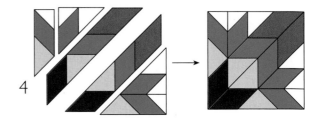

5. Sew quarters into pairs then sew pairs together to complete block. Make six Block A and six Block B. (**Diagram 5**)

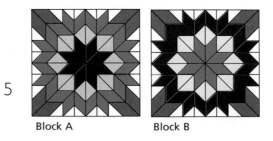

Block A   Block B

FINISHING

1. Place blocks in four rows of three blocks, alternating Blocks A and B. (**Diagram 6**) Sew together in rows then sew rows together.

2. Measure quilt lengthwise. Piece and cut two 2¹/₂"-wide first border strips to that length and attach to sides of quilt.

3. Measure quilt crosswise. Piece and cut two 2¹/₂"-wide first border strips to that length and attach to top and bottom of quilt.

4. Repeat steps 2 and 3 for remaining borders using 4¹/₂"-wide strips.

5 Refer to Finishing Your Quilt, pages 152-153, to complete your quilt.

6

Carpenter's Wheel Quilt Layout

Grandmother's Flower Garden

One of the most popular quilts ever made, the Grandmother's Flower Garden quilt is made up of hexagon shapes most often sewn together by hand. The most popular method of piecing is the English Paper Piecing method in which hexagon shapes are cut out of paper and then basted (or glued with a fabric glue stick) to fabric hexagon shapes. The hexagon shapes are then whip-stitched together.

You can trace the hexagon shape several times onto paper, or you can place a traced shape onto a copier and use it to make the needed number of hexagons for your project. Precut hexagon shapes are also commercially available; check at your local quit store.

See Page 139 for English Paper Piecing techniques.

Springtime Garden

Approximate Size: 71" x 84"

Materials

4³/4 yards white or cream solid

¹/4 yard each of pink solid, pink floral, purple print, green solid

¹/3 yard each of gold, light blue solid, red solid

¹/2 yard each of green print, dark blue solid

²/3 yard light blue print

³/4 yard each red print, dark blue print

¹/8 yard each of orange, orange print and purple solid

freezer paper or cardstock*

glue stick

sewing thread and sharp needle

Check your local quilt shop or use a mail order source to get ready-made templates.

Patterns

A Hexagon

B Partial Hexagon

Cutting

Blocks

Note: *Add ¹/4" for seam allowance around entire template when cutting fabric.*

2266 A, white or cream

22 B, white or cream

62 A, pink solid

2 B, pink solid

125 A, pink floral

2 B, pink floral

92 A, purple print

8 B, purple print

108 A, green solid

121 A, gold

11 B, gold

162 A, light blue solid

168 A, red solid

6 B, red solid

216 A, green print

194 A, dark blue solid

2 B, dark blue solid

324 A, light blue print

339 A, red print

6 B, red print

389 A, dark blue print

2 B, dark blue print

10 A, orange

4 B, orange

22 A, orange print

4 B, orange print

44 A, purple solid

8 B, purple solid

Finishing

2¹/2"-wide bias strips to equal about 350", white or cream

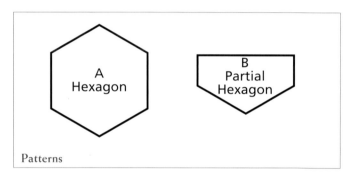

Patterns

Instructions

BLOCKS

1. Referring to English Paper Piecing, page 139, prepare all fabric hexagons.

2. Sew six solid hexagons to a gold hexagon. (**Diagram 1**)

3. Sew a round of twelve print hexagons around the solid hexagons. (**Diagram 2**)

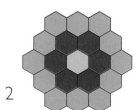

4. Sew a round of 18 cream hexagons to the print hexagons to complete block. (**Diagram 3**)

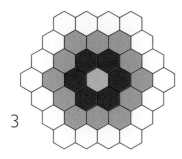

3

5. Repeat steps 2 to 5 for the following blocks (**Diagram 4**):

27 blue
10 pink
18 green
27 red
32 dark blue
1 orange
6 purple

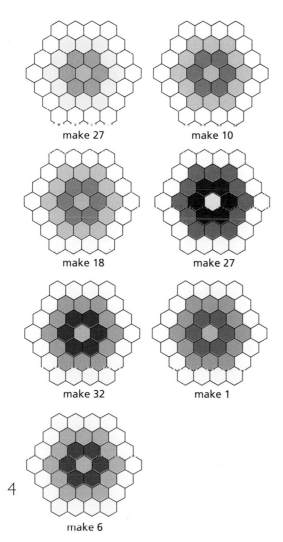

make 27

make 10

make 18

make 27

make 32

make 1

4

make 6

6. For half blocks, sew two solid A hexagons and two solid B shapes to a gold B shape. (**Diagram 5**)

5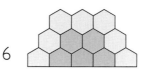

7. Sew two print B shapes and five print A Hexagons to the solid round. (**Diagram 6**)

6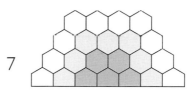

8. Sew two cream B shapes and eight cream A hexagons to the print round to complete the half block. (**Diagram 7**)

7

9. Repeat steps 6 to 8 for the following half blocks (**Diagram 8**):

1 pink
3 red
1 dark blue
2 orange
4 purple

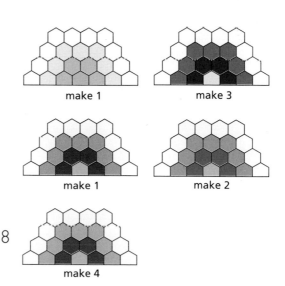

make 1

make 3

make 1

make 2

8

make 4

FINISHING

1. Beginning in the center, sew six pink blocks around a blue block. (**Diagram 9**)

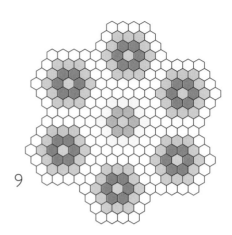

9

2. Continuing sewing rounds of blocks in the following order: green, red, blue, dark blue. (**Diagram 10**)

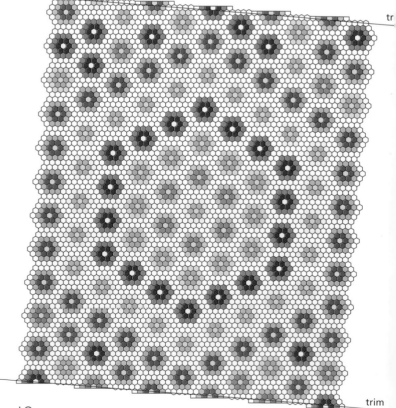

11

4. Trim top and bottom edges. (**Diagram 12**)

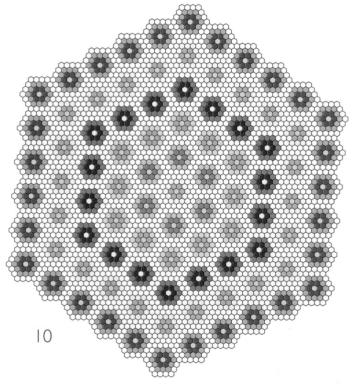

10

3. Fill in corners with remaining blocks and half blocks in random placement. (**Diagram 11**)

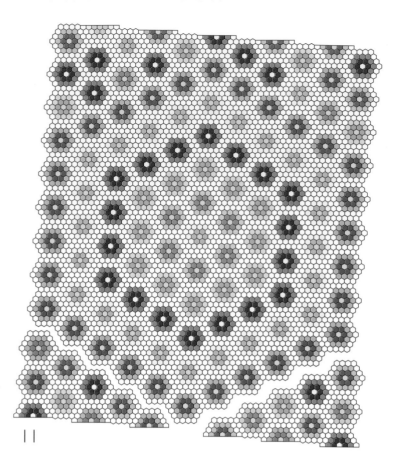

12

5. Sew 2½"-wide bias cream strips together end to end diagonally to make one long strip.

6. Fold in half lengthwise with wrong sides together. Place folded strip along top or bottom edge; sew in place. At corner, fold back away from quilt, then back along next side to be sewn; begin sewing at folded edge.

7. Continue sewing along zigzag edge working bias strips along inner and outer points. **Important:** *Line up binding at inner point of hexagons.*

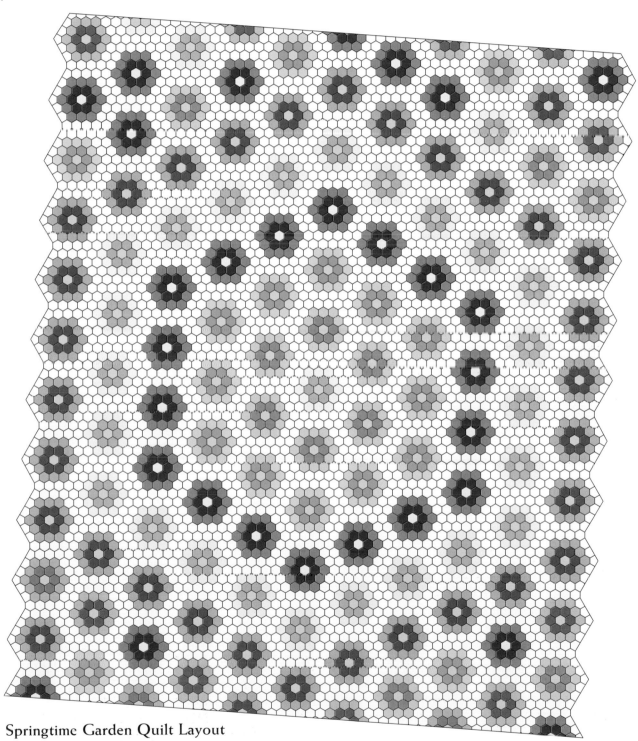

Springtime Garden Quilt Layout

41

Hawaiian Quilt

Hawaiian quilts are a unique combination of both American and Hawaiian cultures. Early in the 19th century when the missionaries first arrived in Hawaii, the Hawaiian women were intrigued watching the missionary wives making quilts. The innovative and creative Hawaiians took these ideas and developed their unique style that more closely represented their own culture. Hawaiian quilt patterns generally do not make use of humans or animals in their designs but rather reflect the Hawaiian love of nature and a profound respect for loved ones.

The quilts usually consist of a large design that is appliquéd onto a background, or several blocks that have a single design appliquéd onto background squares. While the traditional blocks would have been hand appliquéd, this quilt uses the fusible appliqué technique that allows the quilt to be made much easier and faster. If you would like to use hand appliqué, see page 136.

See page 138 for Fusible Appliqué techniques.

Honolulu Fantasy

Approximate Size: 64" x 80"

Materials

1 1/2 yards dark pink batik
1 1/2 yards turquoise batik
2 yards gold batik
2 yards aqua batik
3/4 yard gold batik (first border)
1 1/4 yards dark pink batik (second border)
5/8 yard binding
4 3/4 yards backing
3 yards paper-backed fusible web
Batting

Patterns (pages 180 and 181)

Cutting

Note: *Refer to step 1 of Instructions below to make pattern.*

Blocks

6 Pattern A, aqua batik
6 Pattern B, gold batik
6 squares, 16 1/2" x 16 1/2", dark pink batik
6 squares, 16 1/2" x 16 1/2", turquoise batik

Finishing

6 strips, 3 1/2"-wide, gold batik (first border)
7 strips, 5 1/2"-wide, dark pink batik (second border)
8 strips, 2 1/2"-wide, binding

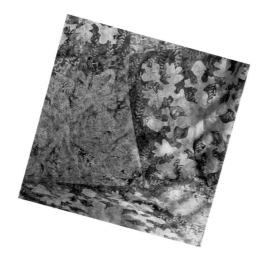

Instructions

BLOCKS

Note: *Read Making a Fusible Appliqué, page 138, before beginning.*

1. The patterns for appliqué designs are given as 1/4 patterns. Trace the pattern onto the paper side of the fusible web. Turn the pattern a quarter turn and place next to the pattern just traced. Trace again. Repeat twice more until the whole pattern is completely traced. (**Diagram 1**)

2. Make six Block A and six Block B. (**Diagram 2**)

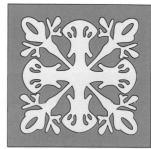

Block A   Block B

2

FINISHING

1. Place blocks according to layout. Sew together in rows then sew rows together.

2. Measure quilt lengthwise. Cut two 3$\frac{1}{2}$"-wide gold batik strips to that length. Sew to sides of quilt. Measure quilt crosswise and cut two 3$\frac{1}{2}$"-wide gold batik strips to that length. Sew to top and bottom of quilt.

3. Repeat step two for second border with 5$\frac{1}{2}$"-wide dark pink batik strips.

4. Refer to Finishing Your Quilt, pages 152-153, to complete your quilt.

Honolulu Fantasy Quilt Layout

Irish Chain

Irish Chain quilts date back to the early 1800s, and there is some uncertainty as to whether they originated in Ireland or America. Although there is little certainty with regards to the origin of quilt patterns, some quilt historians now believe that the Irish Chain pattern was originally created in Ireland and brought to America by an Irish quiltmaker who immigrated to West Virginia in 1807. Whatever its history, the Irish Chain has remained among the most popular of quilt patterns.

Today there are three versions of the Irish Chain: Single Irish Chain, Double Irish Chain and Triple Irish Chain. Each version has "chains" of fabric squares criss-crossing through large open areas.

See page 149 for Strip-Piecing techniques.

Pastel Links

Approximate Size: 58" x 76"

Materials

1 1/2 yards novelty print 1
3/4 yard novelty print 2
1/2 yard pink
5/8 yard blue
1 yard yellow
3/8 yard green
1/2 yard pink (first border)
3/4 yard novelty print 1 (second border)
5/8 yard binding
3 1/2 yards backing
Batting

Cutting

17 squares, 9 1/2" x 9 1/2", novelty print 1
72 squares, 3 1/2" x 3 1/2", novelty print 2
7 strips, 1 1/2"-wide, pink
11 strips, 1 1/2"-wide, blue
18 strips, 1 1/2"-wide, yellow
6 strips, 1 1/2"-wide, green
5 strips, 2"-wide, pink (first border)
6 strips, 4"-wide, novelty print (second border)
7 strips, 2 1/2"-wide, binding

Instructions

BLOCK A

1. For rows 1 and 3, sew 1 1/2"-wide pink strip and a 1 1/2"-wide green strip to opposite sides of a 1 1/2"-wide yellow strip. Press seams toward outer strips. (**Diagram 1**) Repeat for five more strip sets.

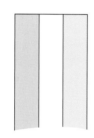

2. For row 2, sew a 1 1/2"-wide yellow strip to opposite sides of a 1 1/2"-wide blue strip. Press seams toward center strip. (**Diagram 2**) Repeat for two more strip sets.

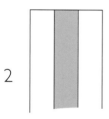

3. Cut strip sets at 1 1/2" intervals until you have a total of 144 strips for rows 1 and 3 and 72 strips for row 2. (**Diagram 3**)

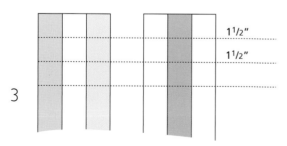

4. Sew rows 1, 2 and 3 together to complete Block A. (**Diagram 4**) Make a total of 72 blocks.

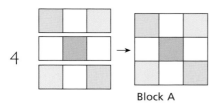

Block A

Hint: *To speed up sewing, chain piece strips. Place row 1 strip right sides together with row 2 strip; stitch. Do not remove from sewing machine. Take another pair of strips and stitch together. Continue sewing rows 1 and 2 until all are sewn. Do not clip apart yet. Take row 3 strip and place right sides together with row 2; stitch. Continue chain piecing row 3 strips until all are sewn. Clip threads apart.*

BLOCK B

1. For rows 1 and 3, sew 1¹/2"-wide blue strip to opposite sides of a 1¹/2" yellow strip. Press seams toward outer strips. (**Diagram 5**) Repeat for another strip set.

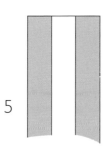

2. For row 2, sew a 1¹/2"-wide yellow strip to opposite sides of a pink strip. Press seams toward center strip. (**Diagram 6**)

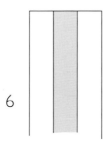

3. Cut strip sets at 1¹/2" intervals until you have 36 strips for rows 1 and 3 and 18 strips for row 2. (**Diagram 7**)

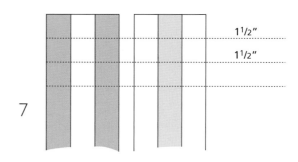

4. Sew rows 1, 2 and 3 together to complete Block B. (**Diagram 8**) Make a total of 18 blocks. Chain piece rows if desired.

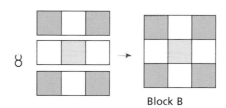

Block B

BLOCK C

1. For rows 1 and 3, sew a Block A to opposite sides of a 3¹/2" novelty print 2 square. Press seams toward square. Repeat for 36 more strips. (**Diagram 9**)

2. For row 2, sew a 3¹/2" novelty print 2 square to opposite sides of a Block B. Press seams toward squares. Repeat for 18 row 2 strips. (**Diagram 10**)

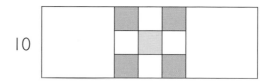

3. Sew rows 1, 2 and 3 together to complete Block C. (**Diagram 11**) Make a total of 18 blocks. Chain piece rows if desired. Blocks should measure 9¹/₂" square.

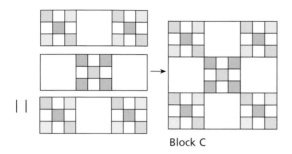

11

Block C

FINISHING THE QUILT

1. Referring to quilt layout, place Block C and 9¹/₂" novelty print 1 squares in seven rows of five blocks.

2. Sew blocks together in rows; press seams for rows in opposite directions. Sew rows together.

3. Measure quilt lengthwise. Piece and cut 2"-wide pink strips to that length; repeat. Sew strips to sides of quilt. Press seams toward border.

4. Measure quilt crosswise. Piece and cut 2"-wide pink strips to that length; repeat. Sew strips to top and bottom of quilt. Press seams toward border.

5. Repeat steps 3 and 4 for second border using 4"-wide novelty print strips.

6. Refer to Finishing Your Quilt, pages 152-153, to complete your quilt.

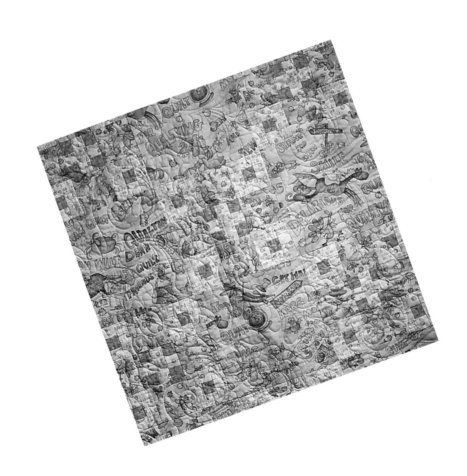

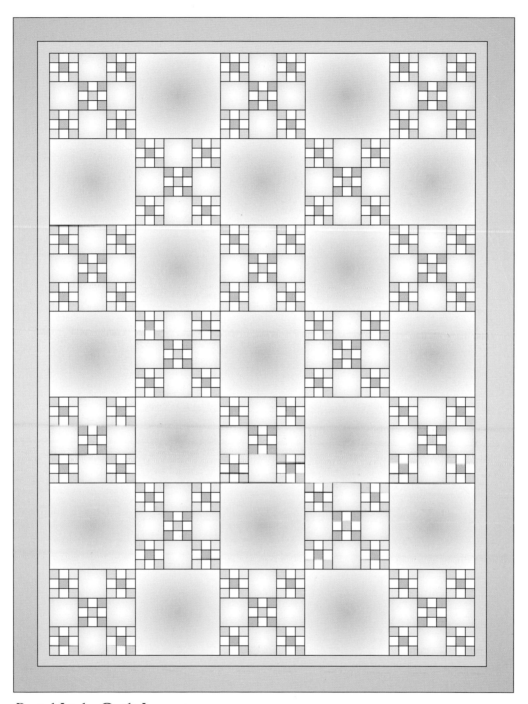

Pastel Links Quilt Layout

Japanese Quilt

For centuries, with both cloth and thread scarce, Japanese peasants used a simple white running stitch to repair worn clothing. A Buddhist priest's robe made around 756 AD demonstrates this technique as it survives today. This simple stitch was the basis of what we know today as Sashiko, a Japanese form of quilting.

By the 18th century the wives of farmers and fisherman were using Sashiko not merely to repair garments but to decorate them as well. The cotton fabric used in these garments was dyed blue using a popular native plant, and by placing two pieces of fabric together, a warm garment was created. To join the two pieces of fabric, running stitches or Sashiko were used.

By the end of the 19th century, Sashiko was no longer considered just a utilitarian device for country folk but became a design feature in the cities as well. Special patterns were popular especially those taken from nature. While Sashiko quilting continued to be used on garments, it gradually began to decorate other things such as quilts.

The quilt shown here is made up of pieced blocks using Japanese print fabrics that were collected on a recent trip to Japan. The alternating plain squares are quilted in the Sashiko style with the cherry blossom pattern. During my trip, I was lucky enough to witness the beauty of the cherry blossoms in full bloom.

See page 148 for Sashiko techniques.

Cherry Blossoms

Approximate Size: 48" x 48"

Materials

Assorted fat quarters Japanese prints,
    red, blue, white, beige, gray, light red
$3/4$ yard dark blue (plain squares)
$1/2$ yard red (first border)
$7/8$ yard blue print (second border)
$1/2$ yard binding
2 yards backing
Batting

Cutting

Blocks

28 squares, $3^7/8$" x $3^7/8$", white
8 squares, $3^7/8$" x $3^7/8$", beige
18 squares, $3^7/8$" x $3^7/8$", red
20 squares, $3^7/8$" x $3^7/8$", blue
4 squares, $3^7/8$" x $3^7/8$", light red
2 squares, $3^7/8$" x $3^7/8$", gray
4 squares, $12^1/2$" x $12^1/2$", dark blue

Finishing

4 strips, $2^1/2$"-wide, red (first border)
6 strips, $4^1/2$"-wide, blue print (second border)
6 strips, $2^1/2$"-wide, binding

Instructions

BLOCK A

1. Cut all white, blue and red $3^7/8$" squares in half diagonally. (**Diagram 1**)

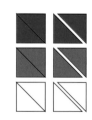

2. Sew a red and a white triangle along diagonal edge; repeat six more times. (**Diagram 2**)

3. Repeat step 2 with blue and white triangles. (**Diagram 3**)

4. Sew a red and blue triangle together; repeat. (**Diagram 4**)

5. Place triangle squares in four rows of four blocks. Sew together in rows then sew rows together. Repeat for a total of four Block A. (**Diagram 5**)

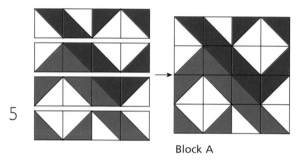

Block A

BLOCK B

1. Cut beige, light red, gray and dark blue $3^7/8$" squares in half diagonally.

2. Sew a beige and blue triangle together. Repeat three more times. (**Diagram 6**)

3. Sew a gray and beige triangle together. Repeat three more times. (**Diagram 7**)

4. Sew a red and beige triangle together. Repeat seven more times. (**Diagram 8**)

5. Place triangle squares in four rows of four blocks. Sew together in rows then sew rows together. (**Diagram 9**)

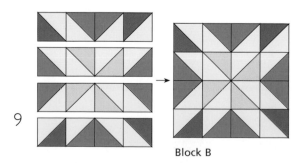

Block B

FINISHING

1. Place Blocks A, Block B and dark blue squares according to layout. Sew together in rows then sew rows together.

2. Measure quilt top lengthwise. Cut two 2½"-wide red border strips to that length. Sew to sides of quilt.

3. Measure quilt top crosswise. Cut two 2½"-wide red border strips to that length. Sew to top and bottom of quilt.

4. Repeat steps 2 and 3 for second border using 4½"-wide blue print strips.

5. Refer to Finishing Your Quilt, pages 152-153 to complete your quilt. **Note:** *Following Sashiko instructions on page 148, hand quilt plain square areas with white quilting thread and Cherry Blossom pattern on page 182.*

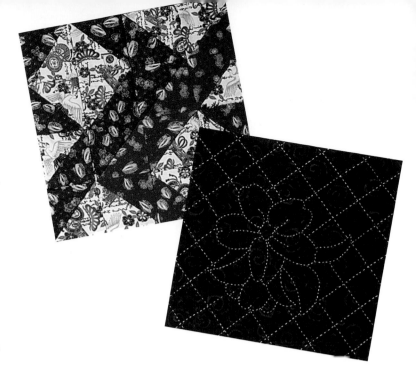

Cherry Blossoms Quilt Layout

Kaleidoscope

Every child is absolutely enchanted when she first looks into a kaleidoscope and sees the ever-changing designs. Imitating a real kaleidoscope, which creates its repeated designs by the use of mirrors, the kaleidoscope quilt consists of blocks with repeated fabric patterns that cause the blocks to magically dance across the surface of the quilt.

A kaleidoscope depends upon mirrors to reflect rays of light. The eye is able to intercept the light and see it reflected many times from the mirror. In a quilt, the fabrics used create the nature of a kaleidoscope's interior on the flat surface of a quilt. Fabrics for kaleidoscope quilts need to be colorful with many different design motifs.

See page 144 for Kaleidoscope techniques.

Fanciful Twirls

Approximate Size: 59" x 59"

Materials

3 yards large floral (includes second border)
1 yard rust
1 yard green
1 yard purple
3/8 yard purple (first border)
5/8 yard binding
3 1/2 yards backing
Batting

Cutting

Blocks

8 repeats, large floral cut into 5"-wide strips
16 squares green, 5" x 5" (cut in half diagonally)
32 strips, green, 2 1/4" x 7 1/4"
16 squares, rust, 5" x 5" (cut in half diagonally)
32 strips, rust, 2 1/4" x 7 1/4"
64 squares, purple, 3" x 3" (cut in half diagonally)

Finishing

4 strips, 2"-wide, purple (first border)
4 strips 4"-wide, large floral (second border)
6 strips, 2 1/2"-wide, binding

Instructions

BLOCKS

1. Carefully place 5"-wide stacked strip on cutting mat. Cut stacked strips into eight squares, 5" x 5". (**Diagram 1**)

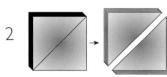

2. Cut stacked squares in half diagonally. (**Diagram 2**) Be sure to keep stacks together.

3. Take a stack of triangles and place on cutting mat so that short edges are at the right and bottom. Measure 1 1/2" from left edge and cut at a 45 degree angle using the 45 degree marking on your acrylic ruler. (**Diagram 3**)

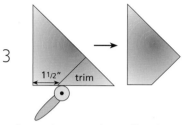

4. Sew a 3" purple triangle to floral triangle along edge just cut. (**Diagram 4**) Repeat for remaining seven triangles in the stack.

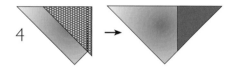

5. Sew floral/purple triangle to rust triangle. (**Diagram 5**) Repeat three more times.

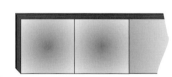

6. Sew 2 1/4" x 7 1/4" rust strip to remaining four floral/purple triangles. (**Diagram 6**) Repeat three more times.

7. Trim rectangles even with diagonal edge of triangles. (**Diagram 7**)

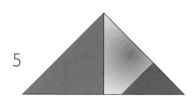

8. Sew triangles from step 5 and step 7 together to make a pieced square. (**Diagram 8**) Repeat three more times.

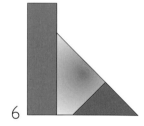

9. Sew pieced squares together in pairs rotating squares as shown. (**Diagram 9**)

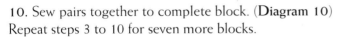

9

10. Sew pairs together to complete block. (**Diagram 10**) Repeat steps 3 to 10 for seven more blocks.

11. Repeat steps 3 to 10 for eight blocks with green background. (**Diagram 11**)

FINISHING

1. Place blocks in four rows of four blocks. Sew together in rows then sew rows together.

2. Measure quilt top lengthwise. Cut two 2"-wide purple border strips to that length. Sew to sides of quilt.

3. Measure quilt top crosswise. Cut two 2"-wide purple border strips to that length. Sew to top and bottom of quilt.

4. Repeat steps 2 and 3 for second border using 4"-wide large floral strips.

5. Refer to Finishing Your Quilt, pages 152-153, to complete quilt.

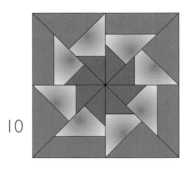

10

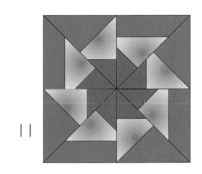

11

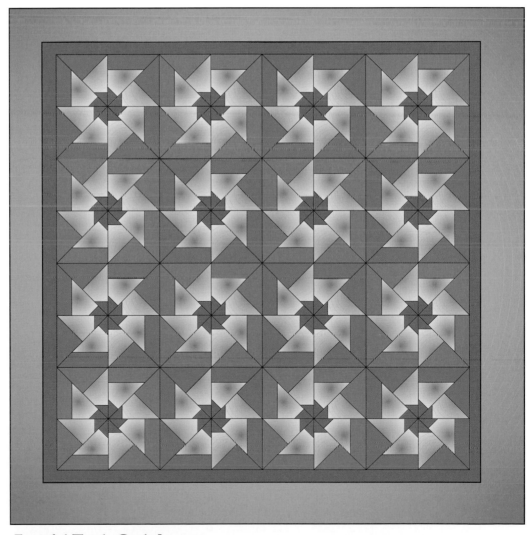

Fanciful Twirls Quilt Layout

Log Cabin

The Log Cabin is among the most recognizable and most loved quilt patterns. It has always been thought of as being the all-American quilt design, but now, there is evidence of the Log Cabin pattern showing up in Europe in the first half of the 19th century and even earlier in ancient Egyptian art.

The traditional Log Cabin block consists of a center square surrounded by light and dark strips.

The center square represents the warmth of a fireplace. The strips surrounding the hearth are the logs of a log cabin house with the light logs representing the light coming in through the window and the dark logs, the dark recesses of the room.

Log Cabins made in the 19th century were usually constructed by sewing strips of scrap fabrics onto a fabric foundation: a method we call foundation piecing today. Later Log Cabins were constructed by the strip-piecing method. Both of these methods are used in this quilt.

See page 140 for Foundation Piecing techniques.

Christmas in the Cabin

Approximate Size: 56" x 56"

Materials

³/₄ yard burgundy (includes border)
1³/₄ yards light green (includes border)
1¹/₂ yards dark green
1¹/₂ yards white/gold
¹/₂ yard binding
3 yards backing
Batting

Pattern (page 183)
Small Log Cabin Block

Cutting

Large Log Cabin Blocks
4 squares, 2¹/₂" x 2¹/₂", burgundy (center)
4 squares, 2¹/₂" x 2¹/₂", white/gold (log 1)
4 strips, 2¹/₂" x 4¹/₂", white/gold (log 2)
4 strips, 2¹/₂" x 4¹/₂", light green (log 3)
4 strips, 2¹/₂" x 6¹/₂", light green (log 4)
4 strips, 2¹/₂" x 6¹/₂", white/gold (log 5)
4 strips, 2¹/₂" x 8¹/₂", white/gold (log 6)
4 strips, 2¹/₂" x 8¹/₂", dark green (log 7)
4 strips, 2¹/₂" x 10¹/₂", dark green (log 8)
4 strips, 2¹/₂" x 10¹/₂", white/gold (log 9)
4 strips, 2¹/₂" x 12¹/₂", white/gold (log 10)
4 strips, 2¹/₂" x 12¹/₂", light green (log 11)
4 strips, 2¹/₂" x 14¹/₂", light green (log 12)

Small Log Cabin Blocks
Note: *The following list shows measurements of the strips needed for piecing the blocks. However, for foundation piecing you do not have to cut exact pieces. Cut strips 2¹/₂" wide, then cut strips as you sew.*

32 squares, 1¹/₂" x 1¹/₂", burgundy (center 1)
32 squares, 1¹/₂" x 1¹/₂", white/gold (log 2)
32 strips, 1¹/₂" x 2¹/₂", white/gold (log 3)
32 strips, 1¹/₂" x 2¹/₂", dark green (log 4)
32 strips, 1¹/₂" x 3¹/₂", dark green (log 5)
32 strips, 1¹/₂" x 3¹/₂", white/gold (log 6)
32 strips, 1¹/₂" x 4¹/₂", white/gold (log 7)
32 strips, 1¹/₂" x 4¹/₂", light green (log 8)
32 strips, 1¹/₂" x 5¹/₂, light green (log 9)
32 strips, 1¹/₂" x 5¹/₂", white/gold (log 10)

32 strips, 1¹/₂" x 6¹/₂", white/gold (log 11)
32 strips, 1¹/₂" x 6¹/₂", dark green (log 12)
32 strips, 1¹/₂" x 7¹/₂", dark green (log 13)

Finishing

8 strips, 2¹/₂" x 14¹/₂", burgundy (first border)
8 strips, 5¹/₂" x 14¹/₂", light green (second border)
6 strips, 2¹/₂"-wide, binding

Instructions

LARGE LOG CABIN BLOCKS

1. Place center square and log 1 right sides together; stitch together. Press seam toward log 1. (**Diagram 1**)

2. Position unit just made with center square at the top. Place right sides together with log 2; stitch. Press seam toward log 2. (**Diagram 2**)

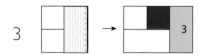

3. Turn unit just made clockwise so log 2 is at the bottom and place right sides together with log 3; stitch. Press seam toward log 3. (**Diagram 3**)

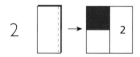

4. Continue adding logs in order until block is complete. (**Diagram 4**) Make a total of four Large Log Cabin blocks.

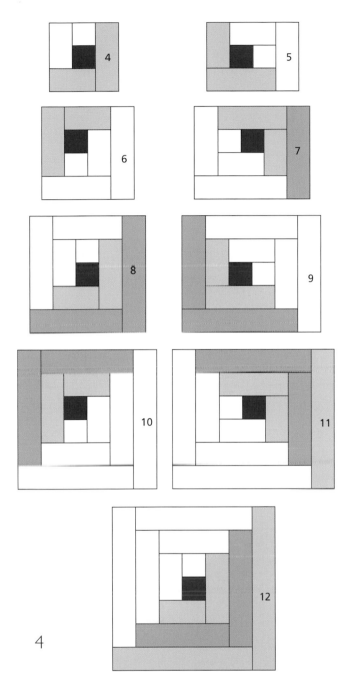

4

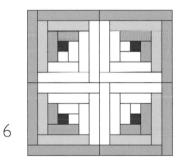

SMALL LOG CABIN BLOCKS

1. Refer to Foundation Piecing, pages 140 to 143, to make 32 Small Log Cabin blocks using $1^{1}/_{2}$"-wide strips. Refer to Cutting above to cut exact strips if desired. (**Diagram 5**)

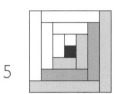

5

FINISHING

1. Sew four small Log Cabin blocks together with white toward center. (**Diagram 6**) Repeat three more times.

6

2. Sew four small Log Cabin blocks together with green toward center. (**Diagram 7**)

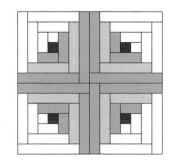

7

3. Place blocks according to **Diagram 8**. Sew together in rows then sew rows together.

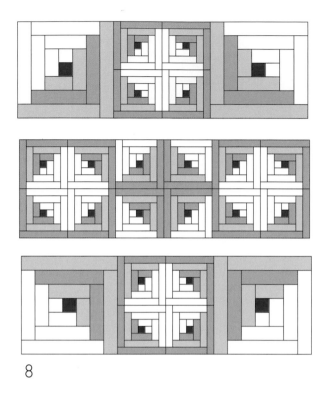

8

4. Sew 2¹/2" x 14¹/2" burgundy strip to 5¹/2" x 14¹/2" light green strip. Repeat seven more times. (**Diagram 9**)

5. Sew two small Log Cabin blocks together with green sides next to each other. Repeat three more times. (**Diagram 10**)

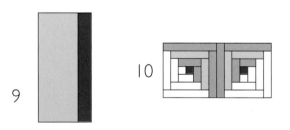

9

10

6. Sew a pieced border strip to opposite ends of small Log Cabin pair. (**Diagram 11**) Repeat three more times to make a total of four pieced borders.

11

7. Sew a border strip to opposite sides of quilt. (**Diagram 12**)

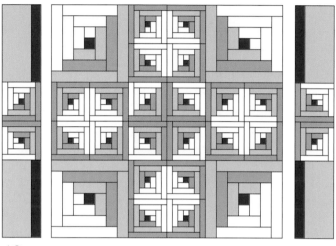

12

8. Sew a small Log Cabin to each end of remaining border strips, then sew to top and bottom of quilt. (**Diagram 13**)

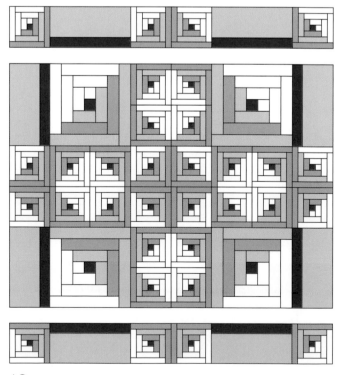

13

9. Refer to Finishing Your Quilt, pages 152-153, to complete quilt.

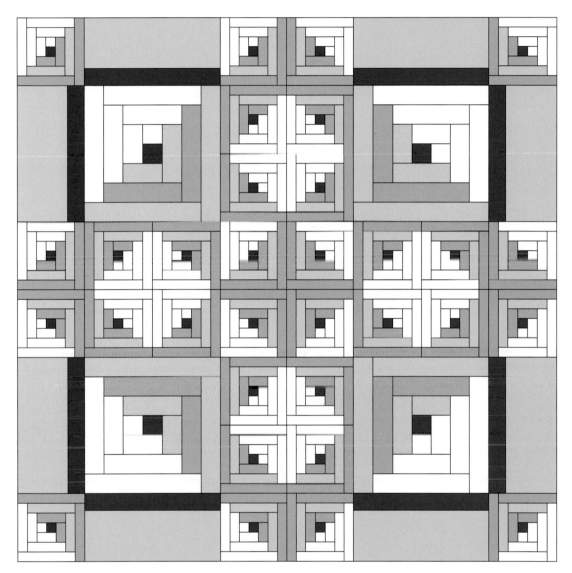

Christmas in the Cabin Quilt Layout

Medallion Quilt

Medallion quilts start with a central motif, and then borders and blocks are added until the desired size and effect is achieved.

This was a very popular quilt style in England during the 19th century where it was sometimes called a "Frame Quilt." The centers were often a special chintz fabric, which was appliquéd to a white cotton background. This technique is called "broderie perse," a French term for "Persian embroidery." Motifs for "broderie perse" were cut from large printed panels often imported into England from India.

American quiltmakers adopted this style for their quilts, often using an elaborate appliquéd block or a square made from a special piece of patchwork for the center. Then borders were created from various patchwork blocks building out to the edge of the quilt.

A medallion quilt is a great way to showcase an elaborate block without having to make a lot of blocks. It is also a great way to practice different quilt techniques.

See page 140 for Foundation Piecing techniques and page 138 for Fusible Appliqué techniques.

Starburst

Approximate Size: 44" x 44"

Materials

¹/₂ yard purple print
¹/₂ yard pink print
¹/₄ yard yellow print
¹/₄ yard gold print
¹/₃ yard dark green
¹/₂ yard medium green
1 yard blue
¹/₂ yard beige
¹/₂ yard pink/yellow print
2 yards backing
¹/₃ yard binding
¹/₂ yard paper-backed fusible web
Batting

Patterns (pages 184 and 185)

Foundation pattern
Flower
Flower Center
Bow Loop
Bow Streamer
Leaf

Cutting

Center Block

Note: *You do not need to cut exact pieces for foundation piecing.*

First Border

2 strips, 1" x 14¹/₂", gold print
2 strips, 1" x 18¹/₂", gold print
2 strips, 2" x 14¹/₂", yellow print
2 strips, 2" x 18¹/₂", yellow print

Second Border

3 strips, 2"-wide, blue
3 strips, 2"-wide, medium green

Triangles

2 squares, 16" x 16", beige
　(cut in half diagonally)
4 strips, 1¹/₂"-wide, dark green

Third border

3 strips, 2¹/₂"-wide, medium green
3 strips, 2¹/₂"-wide, pink/yellow print

Fourth Border

5 strips, 3¹/₂"-wide, blue

Binding

5 strips, 2¹/₂"-wide, blue

Instructions

CENTER BLOCK

1. Read Foundation Piecing, pages 140 to 143, to make four foundation blocks using pattern on page 185. (**Diagram 1**) Note the different placement of the yellow and gold fabric in blocks.

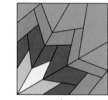

make 2　　　make 2

2. Sew blocks together in pairs, then sew pairs together. (**Diagram 2**)

2

FIRST BORDER

1. Sew 1" x 14¹/₂" gold strip to 2" x 14¹/₂" yellow strip; repeat. Sew to opposite sides of Center Block. (**Diagram 3**)

2. Sew 1" x 18¹/₂" gold strip to 2" x 18¹/₂" gold strip; repeat. Sew to remaining sides of Center Block. (**Diagram 4**)

SECOND BORDER

1. Sew 2"-wide blue strip to 2"-wide medium green strip; press seam to one side. (**Diagram 5**) Repeat with remaining strips.

2. Cut strip set at 2" intervals for a total of 56 pairs of squares. (**Diagram 6**)

3. Sew pairs of squares together to form four patches. (**Diagram 7**)

4.

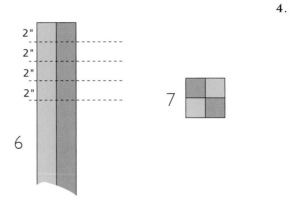

Sew six four patches together; repeat. Sew to opposite sides of quilt. (**Diagram 8**)

5. Sew eight four patches together; repeat. Sew to remaining sides of quilt. (**Diagram 9**)

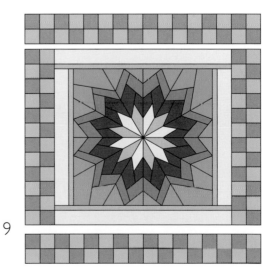

TRIANGLES

1. Cut $1^1/2$"-wide dark green strips in half. Sew strips to adjacent sides of beige triangle. (**Diagram 10**)

2. Trim ends of dark green strips even with diagonal edge of triangle. (**Diagram 11**)

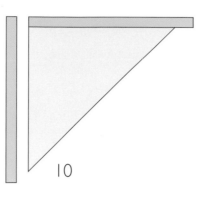

10

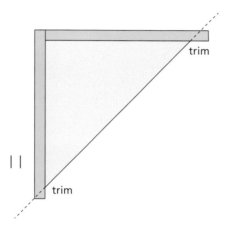

11

3. Sew triangles to opposite sides of quilt top; sew triangles to remaining sides. (**Diagram 12**)

12

4. Trace appliqué patterns from page 184 onto paper side of fusible web. Iron to wrong side of fabrics as noted on patterns. Remove paper backing and fuse to triangles following manufacturer's directions. (**Diagram 13**)

13

THIRD BORDER

1. Cut two medium green squares and two pink/yellow squares from the $2^1/2$"-wide pink/yellow and medium green strips. Sew remaining length of a $2^1/2$"-wide pink/yellow strip to a $2^1/2$"-wide medium green strip. (**Diagram 14**) Repeat with remaining strips.

2. Cut strip sets at $2^1/2$" intervals for pairs of squares. (**Diagram 15**) You will need 38 pairs.

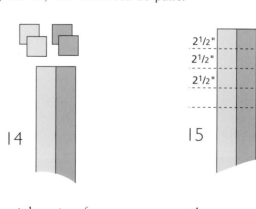

14

15

3. Sew eight pairs of squares; sew a pink square to end of strip. Repeat for another strip. Sew to opposite sides of quilt top. (**Diagram 16**)

16   17   18

4. Sew nine pairs of squares; sew a green square to end of strip. Repeat for another strip. Sew to remaining sides of quilt top. (**Diagram 17**)

FOURTH BORDER

1. Cut two $3^1/2$"- wide blue strips to $38^1/2$" long. Sew to sides of quilt top.

2. Cut two $3^1/2$"- wide blue strips to $44^1/2$" long. Sew to top and bottom of quilt. (**Diagram 18**) **Note**: *If your fabric isn't wide enough, piece border strips diagonally to achieve length.*

FINISHING

1. Refer to Finishing Your Quilt, pages 152-153, to complete quilt.

Starburst Quilt Layout

Nine Patch

The Nine-Patch block was probably the first block little girls learned to make as they were introduced to the craft of quilting. It is a simple, yet versatile block that is made up of nine squares. The squares can be simple squares or more complex squares made up of smaller squares or triangles.

Nine-Patch quilts were developed early in the 19th century. Before the advent of the nine-patch, most quilts were either whole cloth or medallion quilts. Piecing a quilt with small blocks was not only easier and more mobile than working on a large-sized quilt, it also could be made using small bits of scrap fabric during periods when fabric was difficult to find.

While a Nine-Patch block can be made by sewing individual squares together, strip piecing them is easier and much faster.

See page 149 for Strip Piecing techniques.

Squares and Patches

Approximate Size: 63" x 81"

Materials

1/2 yard dark green
1 1/2 yards medium green
5/8 yard purple
1 5/8 yards medium blue
1 1/2 yards light pink
1 1/2 yards light blue
1 1/2 yards light yellow
1/2 yard, light blue (border)
5/8 yard binding
4 yards backing
Batting

Cutting

Block A1

8 strips, 3 1/2"-wide, medium blue
8 strips, 3 1/2"-wide, light blue
2 strips, 3 1/2"-wide, purple

Block B1

8 strips, 3 1/2"-wide, light yellow
8 strips, 3 1/2"-wide, medium green
2 strips, 3 1/2"-wide, dark green
68 squares, 3 1/2"-wide, light pink

Block A2

6 strips, 2"-wide, medium blue
6 strips, 2"-wide, light blue
3 strips, 2"-wide, purple

Block B2

6 strips, 2"-wide, light yellow
6 strips, 2"-wide, medium green
3 strips, 2"-wide, dark green
120 squares, 2", light pink

Strip A3

3 strips, 3 1/2"-wide, medium blue
2 strips, 3 1/2"-wide, light blue

Strip B3

2 strips, 3 1/2"-wide, light yellow
1 strip, 3 1/2"-wide, medium green
28 squares, 3 1/2"-wide, light pink

Finishing

4 squares, 3 1/2", purple
    (for corners of quilt top)
7 strips, 2"-wide, light blue (first border)
8 strips, 2 1/2"-wide (binding)

Instructions

BLOCK A1

1. For rows 1 and 3, sew a medium blue strip to each side of a light blue strip; press seams toward medium blue. (**Diagram 1**) Repeat for another strip set.

2. For row 2, sew a light blue strip to each side of a purple strip; press seams toward purple. (**Diagram 2**)

3. Cut strip sets at 3 1/2" intervals. (**Diagram 3**)

4. Sew rows 1, 2 and 3 together to complete block A1. (**Diagram 4**)

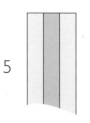
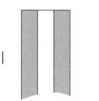

Block A1

5. Repeat steps 1 to 4 for 18 Block A1.

BLOCK B1

1. For rows 1 and 3, sew a light yellow strip to each side of a medium green strip; press seams toward medium green. (**Diagram 5**) Repeat for another strip set.

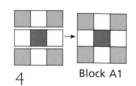

2. For row 2, sew a medium green strip to each side of a dark green strip; press seams toward medium green. (**Diagram 6**)

3. Cut strip sets at 3¹/₂" intervals. (**Diagram 7**)

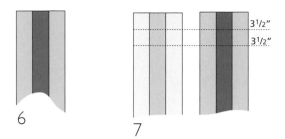

4. Sew rows 1, 2 and 3 together complete nine patch. (**Diagram 8**)

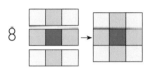

5. Place 3¹/₂" light pink square right sides together with light yellow square of nine patch. Sew diagonally from corner to corner. Trim ¹/₄" from stitching and press back resulting triangle. (**Diagram 9**)

6. Repeat at remaining three corners to complete Block B1. (**Diagram 10**)

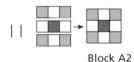

7. Repeat steps 1 to 6 for 17 Block B1.

Block B1

BLOCK A2

Repeat steps 1 to 5 for Block A1 above, substituting 2"-wide strips. Make a total of 30 Block A2. (**Diagram 11**)

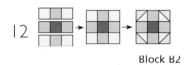

Block A2

BLOCK B2

Repeat steps 1 to 7 for Block B1 above, substituting 2"-wide strips. Make a total of 30 Block B2. (**Diagram 12**)

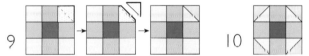

Block B2

STRIP A3

1. Sew a medium blue strip to each side of a light blue strip; press seams toward medium blue. Cut strip set at 3¹/₂" intervals for a total of ten Strip A3. (**Diagram 13**)

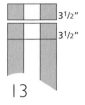

13

STRIP B3

1. Sew a yellow strip to each side of a medium green strip; press seams toward medium green. Cut strip set at 3¹/₂" intervals. (**Diagram 14**)

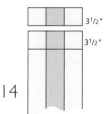

14

2. Place pink square right sides together with yellow square. Sew diagonally from corner to corner of pink square. Trim ¹/₄" from stitching and press back resulting triangle. Repeat on other yellow square to complete Strip B3. (**Diagram 15**) Make a total of 14 Strip B3.

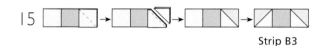

Strip B3

FINISHING

1 Place blocks A1 and B1 alternating in seven rows of five blocks. (**Diagram 16**) Sew together in rows then sew rows together.

16

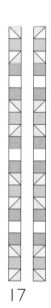

17

2. Sew four strips B3 alternating with three strips A3; repeat. (**Diagram 17**)

3. Sew strips from step 2 to sides of quilt top. (**Diagram 18**)

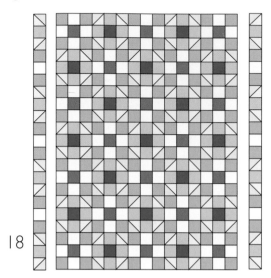

18

4. Sew three Strips B3 alternating with two Strips A3. Sew a 3¹/₂" purple square on each end. Repeat. Sew strips to top and bottom of quilt. (**Diagram 19**)

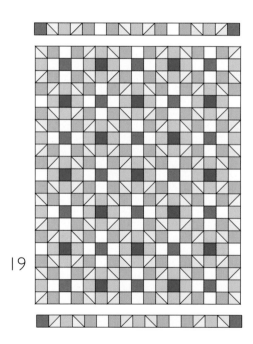

19

5. Measure quilt top lengthwise. It should measure 69¹/₂". Sew and cut 2"-wide light blue strips to that length; repeat. Sew to sides of quilt top. Measure quilt top crosswise. It should measure 54¹/₂". Sew and cut 2"-wide light blue strips to that length; repeat. Sew to top and bottom of quilt top. (**Diagram 20**)

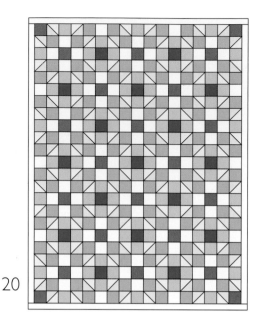

20

6. Sew eight Block A2 and eight Block B2 together, alternating blocks; repeat. Sew to sides of quilt. (**Diagram 21**)

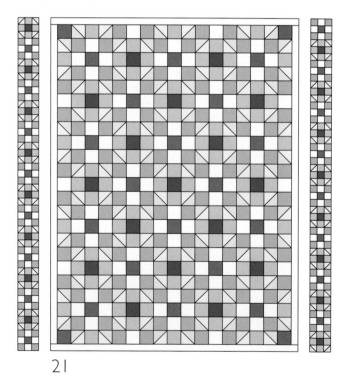

21

7. Sew seven Block A2 and seven Block B2 together alternating blocks; repeat. (**Diagram 22**) Sew to top and bottom of quilt.

8. Refer to Finishing Your Quilt, pages 152-153, to complete your quilt.

22

Squares and Patches Quilt Layout

Ohio Star

The Ohio Star is one of the most recognized star blocks. Because it is so simple to make, it remains one of the most popular. Each block in the quilt is constructed of a center square surrounded by triangles.

Quilt historians are not sure why this block is called an "Ohio Star". It may or may not have originated in Ohio, but many "Buckeyes" have used this pattern to honor their state.

See page 147 for Quarter-Square Triangles and page 148 for Stitch and Flip techniques.

Buckeye Garden

Approximate Size: 60" x 72"

Materials

1/2 yard small floral
1 yard purple swirl
1 yard blue swirl
5/8 yard lavender floral
1/2 yard blue
1/2 yard green
1/2 yard yellow
1/2 yard peach
1 3/4 yards lavender
5/8 yard green leafy print (first border)
1 yard colorful floral (second border)
5/8 yard binding
3 1/2 yards backing
Batting

Cutting

Blocks

20 squares, 4 1/2", small floral
80 squares, 2 1/2", purple swirl
20 squares, 5 1/4", purple swirl
40 squares, 5 1/4", blue swirl
20 squares, 5 1/4", lavender floral
40 squares, 4 7/8", lavender
10 squares, 4 7/8", green
10 squares, 4 7/8", blue
10 squares, 4 7/8", yellow
10 squares, 4 7/8", peach

Finishing

7 strips, 2 1/2"-wide, green leafy
7 strips, 4 1/2"-wide, colorful floral
7 strips, 2 1/2"-wide, binding

Instructions

BLOCKS

1. Place 2 1/2" purple swirl square right sides together with 4 1/2" small floral square. Sew diagonally from corner to corner. Trim fabric 1/4" from stitching and press resulting triangle open. (**Diagram 1**)

2. Repeat step 1 on remaining three corners to complete center square. (**Diagram 2**)

3. Cut all 5 1/4" purple swirl, blue swirl, and lavender floral squares diagonally in quarters. (**Diagram 3**)

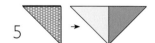

4. Place a blue swirl and a purple swirl triangle right sides together. With blue swirl triangle on top, sew triangles together. (**Diagram 4**)

5. Place a blue swirl and a lavender floral triangle right sides together. With blue swirl triangle on top, sew triangles together. (**Diagram 5**)

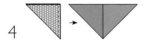

6. Sew pairs of triangles from steps 4 and 5 together to make star points. (**Diagram 6**) Repeat three more times.

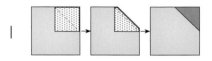

7. Cut all 4 7/8" lavender, green, blue, yellow and peach squares in half diagonally. (**Diagram 7**) Set aside blue, yellow and peach triangles.

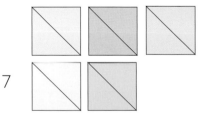

8. Sew a lavender triangle and green triangle together along diagonal edge to make corners. (**Diagram 8**) Repeat three more times.

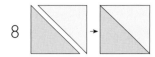

9. Arrange pieced squares from steps 2, 6 and 8 to form a star. (**Diagram 9**)

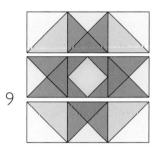

10. Sew squares together in rows then sew rows together to complete Ohio Star block. (**Diagram 10**)

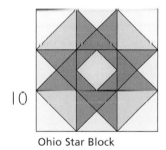

Ohio Star Block

11. Repeat steps 1 to 10 for four more Ohio Star blocks with green corners and five Ohio Star blocks each with blue corners, yellow corners and peach corners. (**Diagram 11**)

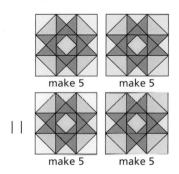

make 5   make 5
make 5   make 5

FINISHING

1. Place blocks in five rows of four blocks; use one of each color in each row.

2. Sew blocks together in rows then sew rows together.

3. Measure quilt lengthwise. Sew and cut $2^{1}/_{2}$"-wide green leafy print strips to that length; repeat. Sew strips to sides of quilt.

4. Measure quilt crosswise. Sew and cut $2^{1}/_{2}$"-wide green leafy print strips to that length; repeat. Sew strips to top and bottom of quilt.

5. Repeat steps 3 and 4 for second border using $4^{1}/_{2}$"-wide colorful floral print strips.

6. Refer to Finishing Your Quilt, pages 152-153, to complete your quilt.

Buckeye Garden Quilt Layout

Postage Stamp

Many of the earliest quilts made in the United States were actually "Postage Stamp" quilts. Because patchwork quilts were originally created from scraps, and fabric was scarce, even the smallest pieces—some no bigger than a postage stamp—needed to be used.

Eventually, the creative quilters began to use those little bits of fabric to create pictorial quilts. They cut the tiny squares individually and then pieced each square one by one, usually sewing the squares together by hand. A masterpiece quilt might contain over 75,000 patches and take about two years to finish.

Now, however, with the invention of the rotary cutting system and gridded fusible interfacing, making a postage stamp quilt is no longer the daunting task it once was. Instead of sewing individual squares, rows of squares are sewn together at the same time.

See page 144 for Postage Stamp techniques.

Petite Sampler

Approximate Size: 26" x 26"

Materials

3/8 yard dark blue
1/8 yard light blue
1/4 yard medium blue
3/8 yard very light blue
1/8 yard aqua
1/4 yard coral
3/8 yard dark red
1/8 yard light red
1/4 yard yellow
1/8 yard gold
1/4 yard pink
1/4 yard gold (first border)
1/4 yard blue (second border)
1/4 yard binding
5/8 yard backing
1 1/2 yards fusible gridded interfacing
    with 1" squares
Batting

Charts (page 86)

Cutting

Blocks

16 squares, 10" x 10", gridded interfacing
288 squares, 1" x 1", dark blue
38 squares, 1" x 1", light blue
199 squares, 1" x 1", medium blue
328 squares, 1" x 1", very light blue
69 squares, 1" x 1", aqua
86 squares, 1" x 1", coral
288 squares, 1" x 1", dark red
54 squares, 1" x 1", light red
86 squares, 1" x 1", yellow
56 squares, 1" x 1", gold
108 squares, 1" x 1", pink

Finishing

2 strips, 1 1/2" x 20 1/2", gold (first border)
2 strips, 1 1/2" x 22 1/2", gold (first border)
2 strips, 2 1/2" x 22 1/2", blue (second border)
2 strips, 2 1/2" x 26 1/2", blue (second border)
3 strips, 2 1/2"-wide, binding

Instructions

BLOCKS

1. On a flat ironing surface, place gridded interfacing square bumpy side up. Position squares referring to the Block Charts on page 85. (**Diagram 1**)

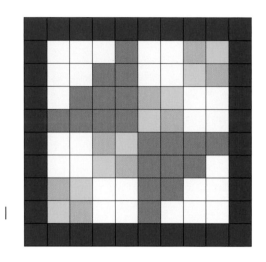

2. Carefully press fabric squares to interfacing referring to manufacturer's directions.

3. Fold last vertical row of squares onto row next to it. (**Diagram 2**)

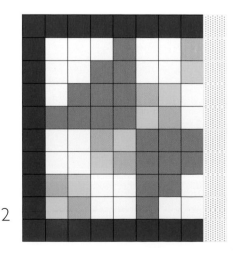

4. Sew using a 1/4" seam allowance. (**Diagram 3**)

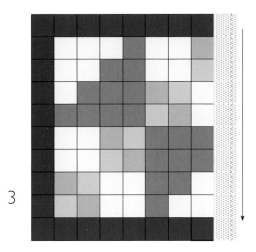

3

5. Continue sewing vertical rows until all are sewn. **Hint:** *Change direction of sewing with each row to keep the block from getting out of shape.* (**Diagram 4**)

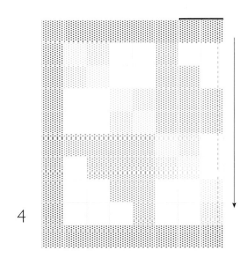

4

6. Snip seam allowance where horizontal rows meet. (**Diagram 5**)

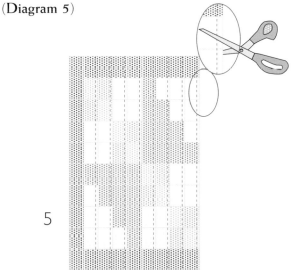

5

7. Press seam allowances for rows in opposite directions. (**Diagram 6**)

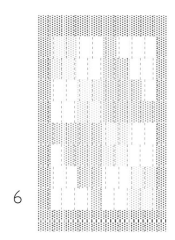

6

8. Sew horizontal rows together to complete block. (**Diagram 7**)

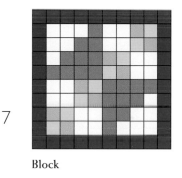

7

Block

9. Repeat steps 1 to 8 for remaining 15 blocks.

FINISHING

1. Place blocks in four rows of four blocks. Sew together in rows then sew rows together.

2. Measure quilt lengthwise. It should measure 20$\frac{1}{2}$". Cut two 1$\frac{1}{2}$"-wide gold strips to that measurement. Sew to sides of quilt.

3. Measure quilt crosswise. It should measure 22$\frac{1}{2}$". Cut two 1$\frac{1}{2}$"-wide gold strips to that measurement. Sew to top and bottom of quilt.

4. Repeat steps 2 and 3 for second border using 2$\frac{1}{2}$"-wide blue strips.

5. Refer to Finishing Your Quilt, pages 152-153, to complete your quilt.

Petite Sampler Block Charts

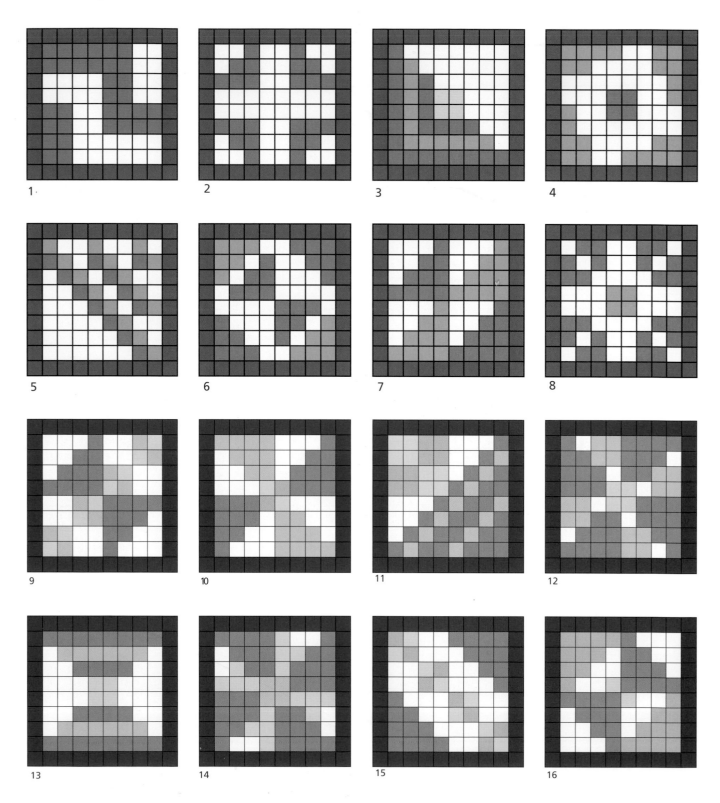

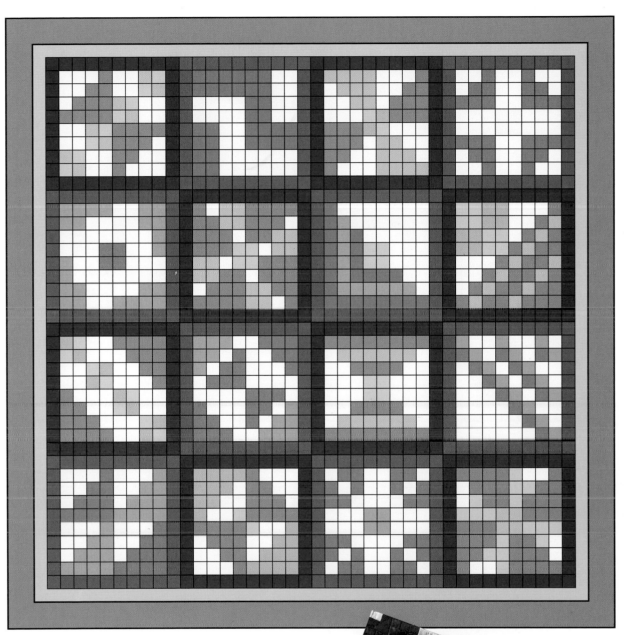

Petite Sampler Quilt Layout

Quarter-Square Triangles

Quarter-square triangles are created when a square is cut diagonally into quarters. They are used most often when the diagonal edge of a triangle is needed on the outside edge of a block (or quilt) to prevent the block or quilt from stretching out of shape.

This motif is simple to make and can add an interesting shape to a quilt design. To make the quarter-square triangles come out even, it is necessary to cut the square larger than the finished square. The general rule is to add $1^{1/4}$" to the finished size of the triangle square. For example, to make a finished 5" finished square, cut the original squares $6^{1/4}$" x $6^{1/4}$".

See Page 147 for Quarter-Square Triangles techniques.

Primitive Pinwheels

Approximate Size: 50" x 50"

Materials

1/2 yard light tan
1/2 yard light/medium tan specs
1/2 yard tan/blue specs
1/2 yard burgundy
1/4 yard green
1/2 yard blue fish print
3/8 yard burgundy (first border)
3/4 yard blue print (second border)
1/2 yard binding
2 1/4 yards backing
Batting

Cutting

Blocks

21 squares, 6 1/4", light tan
8 squares, 6 1/4", light/medium tan specs
11 squares, 6 1/4", tan/blue specs
8 squares, 6 1/4", burgundy
4 squares, 6 1/4", green
12 squares, 6 1/4", blue fish print

Finishing

5 strips, 2"-wide, burgundy (first border)
5 strips, 4"-wide, blue print (second border)
5 strips, 2 1/2"-wide, binding

Instructions

1. Cut all 6 1/4" squares in quarters diagonally. (**Diagram 1**)

2. Sew a burgundy and light tan triangle together along one short side. (**Diagram 2**) Press seam to one side.

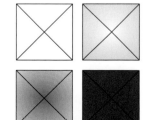

1

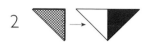

2

3. Sew a blue fish print triangle and light tan triangle together along one short side. (**Diagram 3**) Press seam to opposite side.

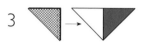

3

4. Sew pieced triangles from steps 2 and 3 together to form a quarter-square triangle. (**Diagram 4**)

4

5. Repeat steps 2, 3 and 4 for remaining quarter-square triangles for a one-quarter section of the quilt. (**Diagram 5**)

make 2 make 2 make 3 make 1
make 1 make 2 make 2 make 1
make 1 make 1

5

6. Place quarter-square triangles according to **Diagram 6**. Sew together in pairs then sew pairs together to form four quarters.

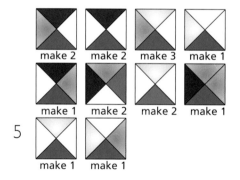

6

7. Sew quarters in pairs then sew pairs together. (**Diagram 7**)

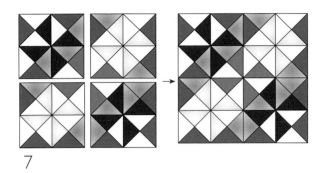

7

8. Repeat steps 2 to 7 for three more quarter sections.

9. Place quarter sections according to quilt layout. Sew quarter sections together in pairs then sew pairs together. (**Diagram 8**)

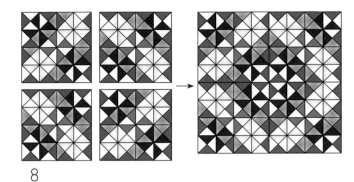

8

10. Measure quilt lengthwise. Sew and cut 2"-wide border strips to that length. Sew to sides of the quilt. Press seams toward border.

11. Measure quilt crosswise. Sew and cut 2"-wide border strips to that length. Sew to top and bottom of quilt. Press seam toward border.

12. Repeat steps 9 and 10 for second border using 4"-wide strips.

13. Refer to Finishing Your Quilt, pages 152-153, to complete your quilt.

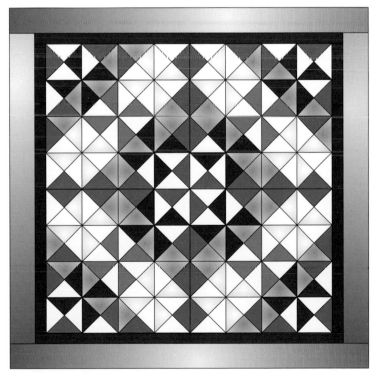

Primitive Pinwheels Quilt Layout

Rotary Cutting

Nothing has done more to popularize quilting than the advent of the rotary cutter. Before this wonderful instrument became available, quilt makers spent long, tedious hours using templates and cutting squares, triangles, rectangles and other shapes individually with scissors. Now, these same pieces can be cut in a fraction of the time.

The rotary cutter—which looks somewhat like a pizza cutter—is used with a protective mat and a strong straight edge, usually an acrylic ruler. The cutter will cut through several layers of fabric, making it easy to cut all of your pieces at the same time. Currently there are many different cutters, mats and rulers on the market. Many of them have many different features, including cost. Once you decide which materials will work best for you, quilt making will become a fast and fun hobby.

See page 146 for instructions on Rotary Cutting techniques.

Stripes and Diamonds

Approximate Size: 59" x 59"

Materials

5/8 yard purple/pink flowers
3/8 yard pink/yellow print
1/4 yard light blue print
1/4 yard green/yellow print
5/8 yard green/yellow flowers
3/8 yard yellow/red print
1/4 yard medium blue print
1/4 yard purple print
1/2 yard medium blue print (first border)
1 1/8 yards zigzag print (second border)
5/8 yard binding
3 yards backing
Batting

Cutting

Purple Block

2 strips, 8 1/2"-wide, purple/pink flowers
4 strips, 2 1/2"-wide, pink/yellow print
2 strips, 2 1/2"-wide, light blue print
2 strips, 2 1/2"-wide, green/yellow print

Green Block

2 strips, 8 1/2"-wide, green/yellow flowers
4 strips, 2 1/2"-wide, yellow/red print
2 strips, 2 1/2"-wide, medium blue print
2 strips, 2 1/2"-wide, purple print

Finishing

6 strips, 2 1/2"-wide, medium blue print
6 strips, 5 1/2"-wide, zigzag print
6 strips, 2 1/2"-wide, binding

Instructions

PURPLE BLOCKS

1. Sew 2 1/2" pink/yellow print, light blue print, another pink/yellow print and green/yellow print strip together. Press seams to one side. Repeat for another strip set, switching positions of light blue print and green/yellow print. (**Diagram 1**)

2. Cut strip sets at 8 1/2" intervals for a total of eight squares. (**Diagram 2**)

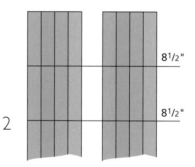

3. Cut squares in half diagonally. (**Diagram 3**)

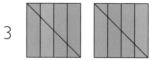

4. Separate triangle in two different stacks. (**Diagram 4**)

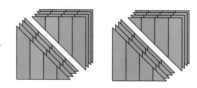

5. Cut 8¹⁄₂" purple/pink flower strips at 8¹⁄₂" intervals to make eight squares. (**Diagram 5**)

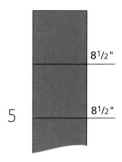

6. Cut diagonally in half. (**Diagram 6**)

7. Sew purple flower triangles to pieced triangles to make pieced squares. (**Diagram 7**) You will need a total of 16 pieced squares (eight of each).

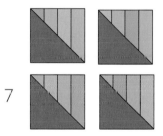

GREEN BLOCKS

1. Sew a 2¹⁄₂" purple print strip, yellow/red print strip, medium blue print strip and another yellow/red print strip. Press seams to one side. Repeat for another strip set switching positions of purple print and medium blue print strips. (**Diagram 8**)

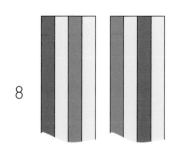

2. Cut strip set at 8¹⁄₂" intervals for a total of ten squares. (**Diagram 9**)

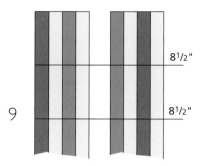

3. Cut squares in half diagonally. (**Diagram 10**)

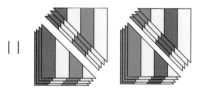

4. Separate triangle in two different stacks. (**Diagram 11**)

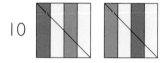

5. Cut 8¹⁄₂" green/yellow flower strips at 8¹⁄₂" intervals to make ten squares. (**Diagram 12**)

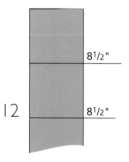

6. Cut diagonally in half. (**Diagram 13**)

7. Sew green flower triangles to pieced triangles to make pieced squares. (**Diagram 14**) You will need a total of 20 pieced squares (ten of each).

14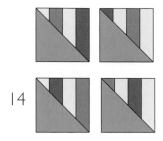

FINISHING
1. Place blocks in six rows of six blocks. Sew blocks together in rows then sew rows together.

2. Measure quilt lengthwise. Piece and cut two $2^1/2$"-wide medium blue print border strips to that length. Sew to sides of quilt top. Measure quilt crosswise. Piece and cut two $2^1/2$"-wide border strips to that length. Sew to top and bottom of quilt top.

3. Repeat step 2 for $5^1/2$"-wide zigzag print border strips.

4. Refer to Finishing Your Quilt, pages 152-153, to complete your quilt.

Stripes and Diamonds Quilt Layout

Stained Glass

Stained Glass quilts are actually pictorial quilts that are intended to resemble stained glass. Narrow black fabric strips that represent the leading in a piece of stained glass surround the pieces. When the entire quilt has been completed, the pieces look as if they have been set in glass.

Many different methods can be used to achieve this look, some more time-consuming than others. For a long time quilters who wanted to make a stained glass quilt were forced to laboriously cut bias strips from black fabric and to affix them to carefully appliquéd pieces. While this traditional technique can still be used, Quick Bias by Clover makes the work easier. This 1/4"-wide pre-folded bias tape is fusible and shapes easily around curves. In the quilt shown, the fabric shapes are cut out and placed onto muslin. The pre-folded bias tape is then used to cover all raw edges. Finally, the tape is stitched down using a machine zigzag stitch and black thread.

See page 138 for Fusible Appliqué techniques.

The Lighthouse

Approximate Size: 22" x 22"

Materials

Scraps, light blue, medium blue, turquoise, aqua, white,
  yellow, red, beige, brown

$1/2$ yard muslin or white fabric

$1/8$ yard red (first border)

$1/4$ yard medium blue (second border)

$3/4$ yard backing

$1/4$ yard binding

$3/4$ yard lightweight paper-backed fusible web

1 package of Quick Bias by Clover

18" x 18" Mylar

Batting

Patterns (pages 186-189)

Cutting

Note: *Trace shapes onto paper-backed fusible web and iron onto desired fabric; cut out fabric pieces along drawn line.*

18" square, muslin

2 strips, $1^{1}/2$" x 16" strips (first border)

2 strips, $1^{1}/2$" x 18", strips (first border)

2 strips, $2^{1}/2$" x 18", strips (second border)

2 strips, $2^{1}/2$" x 22", strips (second border)

3 strips, $2^{1}/2$"-wide, binding

Instructions

BLOCK

1. Using a black permanent marker, trace pattern sections onto Mylar to use as a template for placing pattern pieces. Tape sections together. (**Diagram 1**)
Note: *Pattern is a mirror image to finished project.*

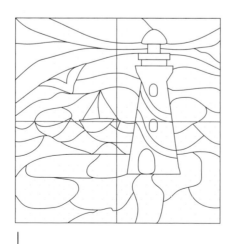

1

2. Place muslin on a flat ironing surface. Flop Mylar template and place it centered on the muslin. Position fabric pieces on the muslin, lifting the mylar as you go. Once all pieces are positioned, remove mylar, fuse in place following manufacturer's directions. (**Diagram 2**)

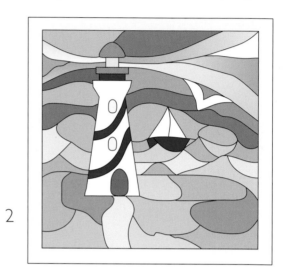

2

3. Place Quick Bias along lines where fabric pieces meet; fuse in place. **Note:** *Place Quick Bias in such a way that raw edges will be covered by another piece of binding.* (**Diagram 3**)

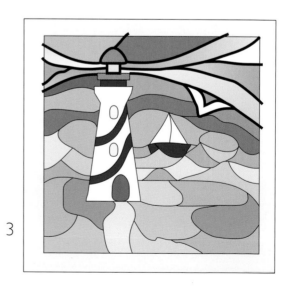

3

4. Sew down with black cotton Quick Bias or smoky invisible thread and using a zigzag stitch large enough to go from edge to edge. (**Diagram 4**)

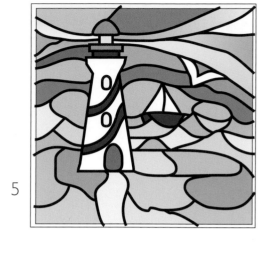

4

FINISHING

1. Trim quilt top to 16" x 16". (**Diagram 5**)

5

2. Sew 1¹/₂" x 16" strips to sides of quilt top; sew 1¹/₂" x 18" strips to top and bottom.

3. Sew 2¹/₂" x 18" strips to sides of quilt top; sew 2¹/₂" x 22" strips to top and bottom.

4. Refer to Finishing Your Quilt, pages 152-153, to complete your quilt.

The Lighthouse Quilt Layout

Templates

Before the advent of rotary cutters, all quilts were made using templates. While the rotary cutter has made cutting squares and triangles with templates obsolete, the use of templates is still necessary for other shapes, such as the ones in a Drunkard's Path quilt. The quilt shown here is a traditional Drunkard's Path, and it has been made with templates.

A template is actually a pattern piece for a particular shape in a quilt. A template can be made of anything from paper to cardboard to plastic. Today there are ready-made acrylic templates on the market. Acrylic templates are easy to handle and can even be used with a rotary cutter.

If you do not have acrylic templates, you can easily make templates following the instructions found on page 150.

See page 150 for Template techniques.

Drunkard's Path

Approximate Size: 74" x 74"

Materials

1¼ yards light pink
⅝ yard dark pink
⅝ yard light green
1¼ yard dark green
⅝ yard yellow
2¾ yards blue
4½ yards backing
⅝ yard binding
Batting

Templates (page 190)

7" Drunkard's Path A and B

Cutting
Blocks
32 A, light pink
16 A, light green
32 A, dark green
16 A, yellow
16 B, dark pink
96 B, blue

Finishing
4 strips, 2½" x 56½", dark green
4 squares, 9½" x 9½", dark pink
8 strips, 2½"-wide, binding

Instructions

DRUNKARD PATH BLOCKS
1. Place a light green A right sides together with blue B matching center points along curved edges. Pin in place at center. (**Diagram 1**)

2. Place a pin at each end of curve. (**Diagram 2**)

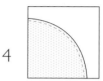

3. Sew curved edges being sure B is on top so you can work with raw edges bringing them together as you sew. (**Diagram 3**)

4. Press seam toward B. (**Diagram 4**)

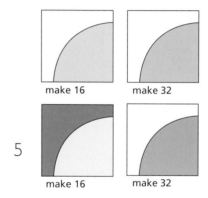

5. Repeat steps 1 to 4 to make remaining Drunkard's Path blocks. (**Diagram 5**)

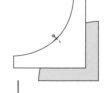

make 16   make 32

make 16   make 32

FINISHING
1. For one quarter of the quilt, place Drunkard's Path blocks according to **Diagram 6**. Sew together in rows then sew rows together.

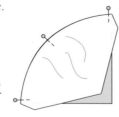

2. Repeat step 1 for three more quarter sections.

3. Sew quarter sections together in pairs then sew pairs together. (**Diagram 7**)

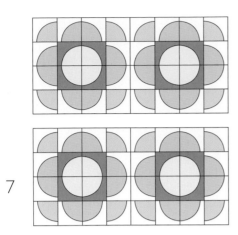

9

7

4. Sew dark green/blue Drunkard's Patch blocks together in pairs. Sew four pairs together to make a border strip. (**Diagram 8**) Repeat for three more border strips

8

5. Sew a Drunkard's Path border strip to a 2¹/₂" x 56¹/₂" dark green strip; repeat three more times. (**Diagram 9**)

6. Sew border strips to opposite sides of quilt. Sew 9¹/₂" dark pink squares to each end of remaining border strips; sew to top and bottom of quilt. (**Diagram 10**)

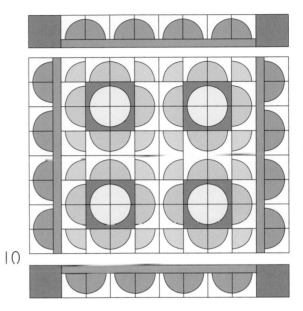

10

7. Refer to Finishing Your Quilt, pages 152-153, to complete your quilt.

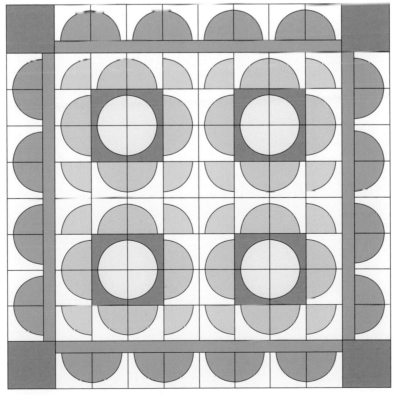

Drunkard's Path Quilt Layout

USA Quilt

The American flag is actually a quilt: the stripes are strip-pieced patchwork, and the stars are appliqué!

Betsy Ross has long been credited with creating the first USA quilt and while Betsy is called a seamstress by most historians, there is no denying that she was also a quilter.

In May 1776, three members of the Continental Congress, George Washington, Robert Morris and George Ross supposedly asked her to sew the first flag. Betsy was certainly known to these gentlemen as her husband was George Ross' nephew, and she worshiped in the pew next to George Washington at Christ Church in Philadelphia.

Did Betsy Ross actually make the first flag? Historically, the story of Betsy Ross is still unsolved, but she remains an interesting figure in the history of the American revolution.

Who made the first flag, however, was certainly a quilter.

See page 146 for Rotary Cutting techniques.

Stars and Stripes

Approximate Size: 82" x 58"

Materials

2 yards red
2 yards white
1¹/2 yards blue
1¹/2 yards gold (includes border and binding)
4 yards backing
1 yard paper-backed fusible web
Batting

Cutting

Blocks

89 squares, 2¹/2" x 2¹/2", red
47 strips, 2¹/2" x 8¹/2", red
3 strips, 2¹/2" x 6¹/2", red
102 squares, 2⁷/8" x 2⁷/8", red (cut in half diagonally)
84 squares, 2¹/2" x 2¹/2", white
42 strips, 2¹/2" x 8¹/2", white
3 strips, 2¹/2" x 6¹/2", white
86 squares, 2⁷/8" x 2⁷/8, white (cut in half diagonally)
1 rectangle, 38¹/2" x 26¹/2", blue
9 squares, 2¹/2" x 2¹/2", blue
10 squares, 2⁷/8" x 2⁷/8", blue (cut in half diagonally)
19 squares, 2¹/2" x 2¹/2", gold
20 squares, 2⁷/8" x 2⁷/8", gold (cut in half diagonally)

Stars

50 stars, white (use with paper-backed fusible web)

Finishing

2¹/2"-wide strips, gold (border)
2¹/2"-wide strips, gold (binding)

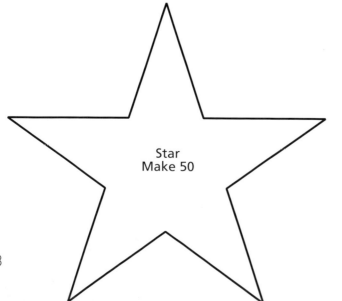

Star
Make 50

Instructions

BLOCK A

1. Sew a red and white triangle together. Repeat three more times. (**Diagram 1**)

2. Sew a 2¹/2" red square, red/white square, 2¹/2" white square and another red/white square together for a pieced strip. Repeat switching positions of red and white squares. (**Diagram 2**)

3. Sew a 2¹/2" x 8¹/2" white strip, a pieced strip (from step 2), a 2¹/2" x 8¹/2" red strip, and another pieced strip together to complete Block A. (**Diagram 3**) Make a total of 33 Block A.

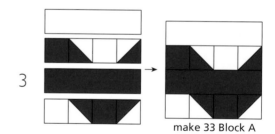

make 33 Block A

BLOCK B

1. Sew a red and a white triangle together. Repeat three more times. (**Diagram 4**)

2. Sew a red/white square to opposite sides of a 2¹/2" white square. Sew a red/white square to opposite sides of a 2¹/2" red square. (**Diagram 5**)

3. Sew a 2$\frac{1}{2}$" x 6$\frac{1}{2}$" white strip, pieced strip (from step 2), 2$\frac{1}{2}$" x 6$\frac{1}{2}$" red strip and another pieced strip together to complete Block B. (**Diagram 6**) Repeat for another Block B.

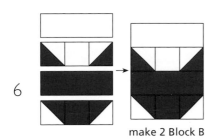

make 2 Block B

BLOCK C

1. Sew a red and a white triangle together; repeat. Sew a red and a gold triangle together; repeat. (**Diagram 7**)

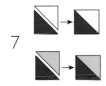

2. Sew a 2$\frac{1}{2}$" red square, red/white square, 2$\frac{1}{2}$" white square and another red/white square together. Sew a 2$\frac{1}{2}$" gold square, red/gold square, 2$\frac{1}{2}$" red square and another red/gold square. (**Diagram 8**)

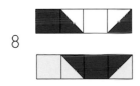

3. Sew 2$\frac{1}{2}$" x 8$\frac{1}{2}$" white strip, red/white pieced strip, 2$\frac{1}{2}$" x 8$\frac{1}{2}$" red strip and red/gold pieced strip together to complete Block C. (**Diagram 9**)

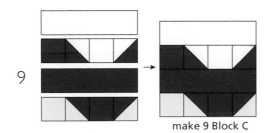

make 9 Block C

BLOCK D

1. Sew a gold and red triangle together; repeat. Sew a white and red triangle together; repeat. (**Diagram 10**)

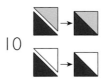

2. Sew a 2$\frac{1}{2}$" red square, red/gold square, 2$\frac{1}{2}$" gold square and red/gold square together to form a pieced strip. Sew a 2$\frac{1}{2}$" white square, red/white square, 2$\frac{1}{2}$" red square, and red/white square together. (**Diagram 11**)

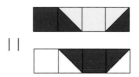

3. Sew the red/gold pieced strip, a 2$\frac{1}{2}$" x 8$\frac{1}{2}$" red strip and a red/white strip together to complete Block D. (**Diagram 12**)

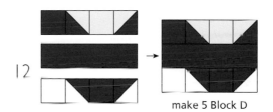

make 5 Block D

BLOCK E

1. Sew a red and a white triangle together; repeat. Sew a red and a gold triangle together; repeat. (**Diagram 13**)

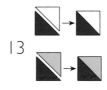

2. Sew a red/white square, 2$\frac{1}{2}$" white square and another red/white square together. Sew a red/gold square, 2$\frac{1}{2}$" red square and another red/gold square. (**Diagram 14**)

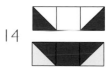

U is for USA Quilt

3. Sew 2¹/₂" x 8¹/₂" white strip, red/white pieced strip, 2¹/₂" x 8¹/₂" red strip and red/gold pieced strip together to complete Block E. (**Diagram 15**)

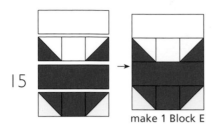

15

make 1 Block E

STRIPS F, G, H, AND I

1. Sew a gold and a blue triangle together; repeat for a total of ten blue/gold squares. Sew a white and blue triangle together; repeat for a total of ten blue/white squares. (**Diagram 16**)

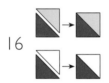

16

2. Sew a blue/gold square to opposite sides of a 2¹/₂" gold square; repeat four more times. Sew a 2¹/₂" blue square to one end of four of the pieced strips. These are Strips F and G. (**Diagram 17**)

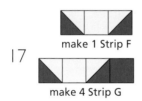

17

make 1 Strip F

make 4 Strip G

3. Repeat steps 1 and 2 using blue and white triangles and squares to complete Strips H and I. (**Diagram 18**)

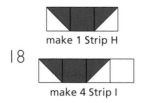

18

make 1 Strip H

make 4 Strip I

FINISHING

1. Sew five Block D together. Sew five Block A together; repeat for four more rows. Sew five Block C together. Sew the rows together making sure the gold is at the top and bottom. (**Diagram 19**)

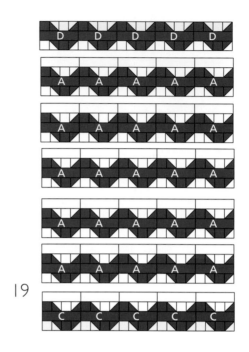

19

2. Sew a Block B and four Block A; repeat. Sew a Block E and four Block C. Sew the rows together making sure the gold is at the bottom. (**Diagram 20**)

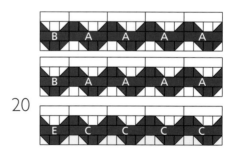

20

3. Sew one Strip F and four Strip G together; sew one Strip H and four Strip I. Sew pieced strips to the 38¹/₂" x 26¹/₂" blue rectangle. (**Diagram 21**)

21

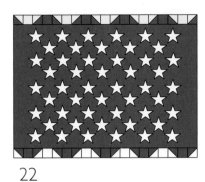

22

23

4. Trace Star pattern 50 times onto paper-backed fusible web; fuse to wrong side of white fabric and cut out. Position stars on blue rectangle section and fuse in place. (**Diagram 22**) Finish edges of stars with machine zigzag and white thread.

5. Sew the three sections together. (**Diagram 23**)

6. Measure the quilt lengthwise; cut two 2$\frac{1}{2}$"-wide gold border strips to that length. Sew to sides of the quilt. Measure the quilt crosswise; cut two 2$\frac{1}{2}$"-wide gold border strips to that length. Sew to top and bottom of quilt.

7. Refer to Finishing Your Quilt, pages 152-153, to complete your quilt.

Stars and Stripes Quilt Layout

Vintage Quilt

Vintage quilts show up in the strangest places: antique shops, flea markets, garage sales—even on ebay®. They are quilts made in the last part of the 19th and the first part of the 20th centuries. Occasionally they are complete quilts and sometimes—as in the case of this quilt—only pieces. There were 63 blocks carefully pieced and then forgotten by an unknown quiltmaker, which I joined together to make this quilt. Because some of the current fabric manufacturers are producing vintage fabrics, I was able to add a border that compliments the quilt.

This quilt pattern, Monkey Wrench, was used as a code on the Underground Railroad to signal fleeing slaves. According to tradition, ten different quilts served to direct slaves to take particular actions. Each quilt featured one of the ten patterns, and the ten quilts were placed, one at a time, on a fence. Since it was common for quilts to be aired out frequently, the master or mistress would not be suspicious when the quilts were displayed on the fence. Each quilt served as a non-verbal communication for the fleeing slave.

The Monkey Wrench block, which symbolized a tool, indicated that the time was ripe to gather up the tools—both actual and spiritual—which would be needed for the long, dangerous journey ahead.

See page 146 for Rotary Cutting techniques.

Monkey Wrench

Approximate Size: 82" x 100"

Materials

Fat quarters of assorted light (A) and dark
   or medium (B) fabrics*
$5/8$ yard green (first border)
1 yard red print (second border)
$1 5/8$ yards blue print (third border)
1 yard binding
7 yards backing
Batting
Use assorted fat quarters if you would like a scrappy look like the photographed quilt. You can make four blocks from two fat quarters—one light and one dark.

Cutting

For each Block
2 squares, $4^{3}/8$", fabric A
2 squares, $4^{3}/8$", fabric B
1 square, $2^{1}/2$", fabric A
4 rectangles, $2^{1}/4$" x $2^{1}/2$", fabric A
4 rectangles, $2^{1}/4$" x $2^{1}/2$", fabric B

For entire quilt
126 squares, $4^{3}/8$", fabric A
126 squares, $4^{3}/8$", fabric B
63 squares, $2^{1}/2$", fabric A
*252 rectangles, $2^{1}/4$" x $2^{1}/2$", fabric A
*252 rectangles, $2^{1}/4$" x $2^{1}/2$", fabric B
If using a single fabric for fabric A and a single fabric for fabric B, you can cut strips, $2^{1}/4$"-wide and sew a fabric A and fabric B strip together; then cut at $2^{1}/2$" intervals for pairs of rectangles already sewn.

Finishing
9 strips, 2"-wide, green (first border)
9 strips, $3^{1}/2$"-wide, red print (second border)
10 strips, $5^{1}/2$"-wide, blue print (third border)
10 strips, $2^{1}/2$"-wide (binding)

Instructions

MONKEY WRENCH BLOCK
1. Cut all A and B $4^{3}/8$" squares in half diagonally. (**Diagram 1**)

2. Sew a fabric A and fabric B triangle together along diagonal edge to make a triangle square. Repeat three more times. (**Diagram 2**)

  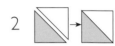

3. If using individual rectangles, sew a dark and a light rectangle together along the $2^{1}/2$" edge. Repeat three more times. (**Diagram 3**)

If using strips, sew fabric A and fabric B strip together; press seam to one side. Cut strip set at $2^{1}/2$" intervals. Repeat for a total of 252 pairs of squares. (**Diagram 4**)

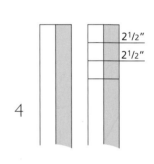

4. Place triangle squares, rectangle pairs and $2^{1}/2$" square according to **Diagram 5**. Sew together in rows then sew rows together.

5. Repeat for remaining 62 blocks.

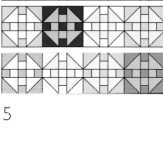

5

FINISHING

1. Place blocks in nine rows of seven blocks. Sew blocks together in rows then sew rows together.

2. Measure quilt top lengthwise. Sew and cut 2"-wide green strips to that length; repeat. Sew to sides of quilt. Measure quilt crosswise. Sew and cut 2"-wide green strips to that length. Sew to top and bottom of quilt.

3. Repeat step 2 for second and third borders using 3½"-wide red print strips and 5½"-wide blue print strips.

4. Refer to Finishing Your Quilt, pages 152-153, to complete your quilt.

Monkey Wrench Quilt Layout

Watercolor Quilt

The concept of the watercolor quilt was originated by the English quilt artist, Deirdre Amdsen, who first conceived of the idea of treating printed fabrics as color gradations. The technique mimics the Impressionist School of painting where small dots of color combine to present the picture. Instead of paint, the quilter builds the picture with little squares of fabric (usually about 2 inches). The fabrics merge and form a new image just as the small dots of paint do. The choice of fabrics and which fabrics are placed next to each other is essential so that the eye can blend these little squares into the image.

The introduction of fusible gridded interfacing made creating watercolor quilts an easier project. The squares of fabric are placed on the interfacing following a chart that is similar to a cross-stitch chart. Working in smaller sections makes the stitching easier to do. Some of the colors listed may be part of the same fabric. For example, light green and light pink may appear in the same fabric.

See page 151 for Watercolor techniques.

Butterfly Garden

Approximate Size: 63" x 75"

Materials

¹/₄ yard black
³/₈ yard dark orange
¹/₄ yard light orange
³/₈ yard gold
¹/₄ yard dark yellow
¹/₈ yard light yellow
¹/₄ yard blue floral
¹/₄ yard purple floral
³/₄ yard dark pink floral
³/₈ yard light pink floral
³/₈ yard multi-color floral
¹/₈ yard blue/multi-color
³/₈ yard blue/yellow
1¹/₂ yards blue/pink rosebud (background)
1¹/₈ yards blue/pink (border)
1¹/₈ yards blue floral (border)
⁵/₈ yard dark blue floral (border)
6 yards fusible gridded interfacing
4 yards backing
⁵/₈ yard binding
Batting

Cutting

Cut the following 2" squares:
9 black
72 dark orange
48 light orange
65 gold
37 dark yellow
16 light yellow
30 blue floral
35 purple floral
237 dark pink floral
74 light pink floral
68 multi-color floral
43 blue/multi-color
59 blue/yellow
468 blue/pink rosebud (background)
328 blue/pink (border)
347 blue floral (border)
164 dark blue floral (border)

Instructions

1. Cut interfacing into ten 22" x 20" sections and ten 20" x 20" sections.

2. Using the charts on page 191, and working with one section at a time, place squares of fabric onto fusible gridded interfacing; press to fuse following manufacturer's directions. (**Diagram 1**)

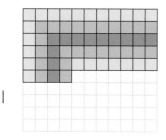

2. Sew rows of squares together. Fold last vertical row onto row next to it; sew with a ¹/₄" seam allowance. (**Diagram 2**)

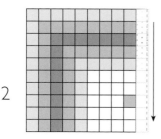

3. Sew remaining vertical rows in same manner changing direction of sewing with each row. (**Diagram 3**)

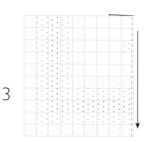

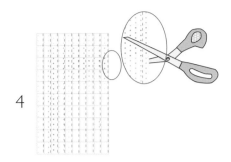

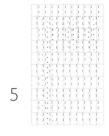

4

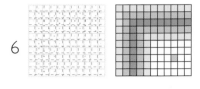

5

6

4. Snip seam allowances at each point where rows meet. (**Diagram 4**)

5. Press seams for rows in alternating directions. (**Diagram 5**)

6. Sew horizontal rows in same manner until section is complete. (**Diagram 6**) Repeat for remaining sections.

FINISHING

1. Place sections according to Layout.

2. Sew sections together in rows then sew rows together.

3. Refer to Finishing Your Quilt, pages 152-153, to complete your quilt.

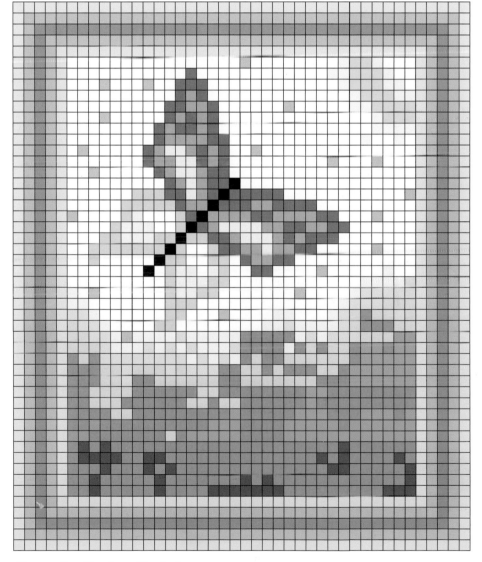

Butterfly Garden Quilt Layout

X-ray

We all know that x-rays are used to find things we can't always see with the naked eye. Sometimes looking at quilts, we first see one pattern emerging, but soon after looking further we see another pattern. Our eyes have become X-Ray machines.

What if the X-Ray was built into the quilt? Look at the upper left of the photographed quilt. You see a simple mosaic pattern. Now look at the "X-Ray" of the lower right of the quilt, and a whole new pattern emerges: rows of dark wavy lines with triangle squares dancing in between.

Want to get rid of the X-Ray? Make the entire quilt with Block A and don't use the gray and black fabric in the border.

See page 147 for Half-Square Triangle techniques.

Another View

Approximate Size: 78" x 90"

Materials

5/8 yard light turquoise

1/2 yard medium turquoise

3/4 yard dark turquoise

5/8 yard light peach stars

3/4 yard dark peach

5/8 yard light gray

1/2 yard medium gray

5/8 yard dark gray stars

3/4 yard black 1

3/4 yard black 2

1/2 yard each dark turquoise and black 1 (first border)

1 yard each light peach stars and dark gray stars
    (second border)

1/2 yard each medium gray and medium turquoise
    (binding)

7 yards backing

Batting

Cutting

Block A

24 squares, 3^1/$_2$", dark turquoise

24 squares, 3^1/$_2$", dark peach

36 squares, 3^7/$_8$", light turquoise

24 squares, 3^7/$_8$", medium turquoise

24 squares, 3^7/$_8$", dark turquoise

36 squares, 3^7/$_8$", light peach

24 squares, 3^7/$_8$", dark peach

Block B

24 squares, 3^1/$_2$", black 1

24 squares, 3^1/$_2$", black 2

36 squares, 3^7/$_8$", light gray

24 squares, 3^7/$_8$", medium gray

24 squares, 3^7/$_8$", black 1

36 squares, 3^7/$_8$", dark gray stars

24 squares, 3^7/$_8$", black 2

Finishing

4 strips, 3^1/$_2$"-wide, dark turquoise (first border)

4 strips, 3^1/$_2$"-wide, black 1 (first border)

5 strips, 6^1/$_2$"-wide, light peach stars (second border)

5 strips, 6^1/$_2$"-wide, dark gray stars (second border)

2 squares, 6^1/$_2$" x 6^1/$_2$", dark peach

2 squares, 6^1/$_2$" x 6^1/$_2$", black 2

5 strips, 2^1/$_2$"-wide, medium gray (binding)

5 strips, 2^1/$_2$"-wide, medium turquoise (binding)

Instructions

BLOCK A

1. Referring to Half-Square Triangles, page 147, cut all the 3^7/$_8$" light turquoise, medium turquoise, dark turquoise, light peach, and dark peach squares diagonally in half. (**Diagram 1**)

2. Place a dark peach triangle right sides together with a light turquoise triangle; sew along diagonal edge to make a half square triangle. Repeat two more times. (**Diagram 2**)

3. Make remaining half square triangles using the following pairs: light turquoise and dark turquoise, light peach and medium turquoise, light peach and dark peach, and light peach and dark turquoise. (**Diagram 3**)

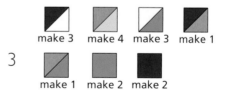

4. Place half square triangles and squares referring to Diagram 4.

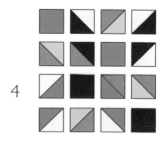

5. Sew together in rows. Press seams for rows in opposite directions. Sew rows together to complete Block A. (**Diagram 5**) Make a total of 12 Block A.

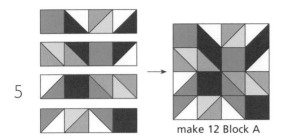

5

make 12 Block A

BLOCK B

1. Cut all the 3⅞" light gray, medium gray, dark gray stars, black 1 and black 2 squares diagonally in half. (**Diagram 6**)

lt gray   dk gray   black 1

6

med gray   black 2

2. Place a black 1 triangle right sides together with a light gray triangle; sew along diagonal edge to make a half square triangle. Repeat two more times. (**Diagram 7**)

7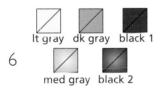

3. Make remaining half square triangles using the following pairs: light gray and black 2, dark gray and medium gray, light gray and black 1, medium gray and black 2, and medium gray and black 1.(**Diagram 8**)

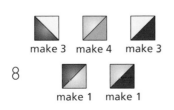

make 3   make 4   make 3

8

make 1   make 1

4. Place half square triangles and squares referring to **Diagram 9**.

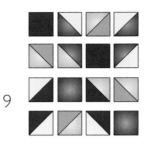

9

5. Sew together in rows. Press seams for rows in opposite directions. Sew rows together to complete Block B. (**Diagram 10**) Make a total of 12 Block B.

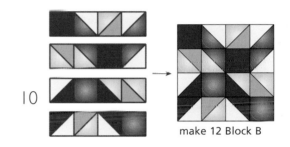

10

make 12 Block B

FINISHING

1. Place Blocks A and B according to quilt layout. Sew together in rows. Press seams for rows in opposite directions. Sew rows together.

2. Measure quilt lengthwise. Sew $3^1/2$"-wide black 1 and $3^1/2$" dark turquoise strips together diagonally to that length. Cut border strip so that seam between dark turquoise and black strip matches seam between Block A and Block B. (**Diagram 11**) Repeat. Sew to sides of quilt. Trim border at each end. (**Diagram 12**)

3. Measure quilt crosswise. Sew and cut $3^1/2$" dark turquoise strip to that length. Sew to top of quilt. Repeat with $3^1/2$" black 1 strip for bottom of quilt.

4. Repeat step 2 with $6^1/2$"-wide light peach stars and dark gray stars border strips.

5. Measure quilt crosswise. Sew and cut $6^1/2$"-wide light peach strips and $6^1/2$"-wide dark gray strips to that length. Sew $6^1/2$" dark peach squares to each end of light peach strips and $6^1/2$" black 2 squares to each end of dark gray strips. (**Diagram 13**) Sew to top and bottom of quilt.

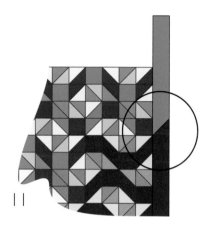

11

trim.

trim

12

13

6. Refer to Finishing Your Quilt, pages 152-153, to complete quilt.

Note: *Piece the binding using two separate strips. Begin and end light turquoise strip on the colored portion of the quilt, leaving at least a 4" tail at each end. Repeat with the light gray strip on the x-ray portion of the quilt. Referring to Attaching the Continuous Machine Binding, page 152, finish the binding at both ends.*

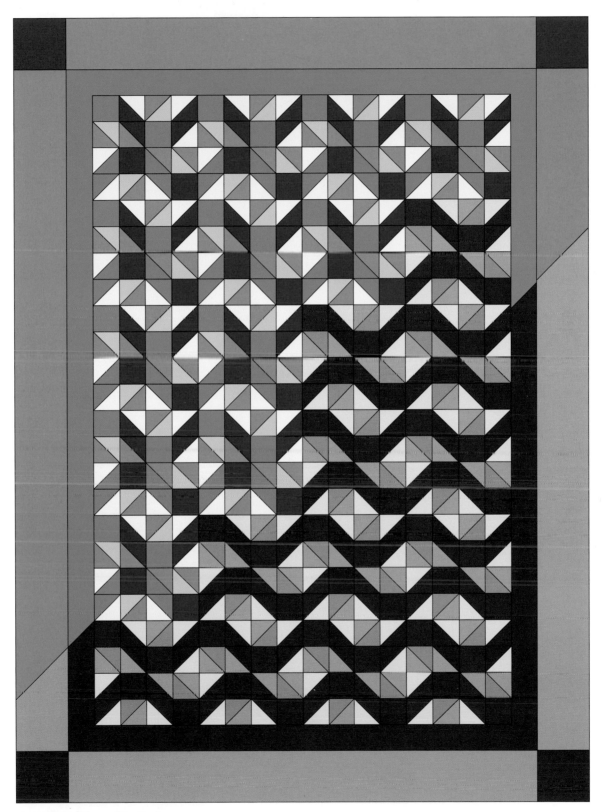

Another View Quilt Layout

Yo-Yo Quilt

If you think of a quilt as three layers quilted together, then the Yo-Yo is technically not a quilt. Yet, several definitive books on the history of American quilts include them because they were such popular bed coverings in the 1920s and 1930s

Traditional quilt makers might very well turn away from a Yo-Yo quilt, but a quilt made from Yo-Yo's—those puffy little circles—has always been fun to make. The Yo-Yo is easy to cut, quick to make, and requires no special talent. In addition, it can be made from any combination of scraps, but the results can be quite enchanting

Anyone looking for fun with fabric that allows you to start a project that is easy to finish will certainly enjoy making a Yo-Yo Quilt.

See page 151 for Yo-Yo techniques.

Colorful Coverlet

Approximate Size: 36³/₄" x 49"

Materials

Assorted fabric scraps, light, medium and dark
Sewing thread and needles

Template

4" circle

Cutting

156 circles, dark
288 circles, medium
144 circles, light

Yo Yo Pattern
4" Circle

Instructions

YO-YO BLOCKS

1. Make all cut circles into yo-yos referring to Making a Yo-Yo, page 151. The 4" circle will make a yo-yo that finishes about 1³/₄" in diameter.

2. Place yo-yos in seven rows of seven referring to **Diagram 1.**

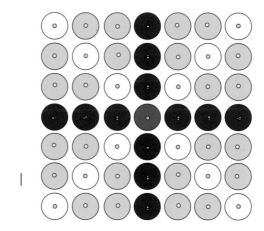

3. Sew two yo-yos together using five or six stitches. (**Diagram 2**)

4. Continue to sew yo-yos in rows. (**Diagram 3**)

5. Sew rows together to complete a yo-yo block. (**Diagram 4**) Make 11 more blocks.

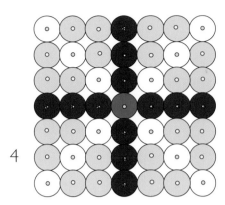

4

FINISHING
Sew blocks together in rows, then sew rows together to complete yo-yo quilt.

Colorful Coverlet Layout

Zigzag Quilt

There is probably no quilt easier to make than a quilt made entirely of the Zigzag block. Just make five differently colored squares joined with black, cut into triangles, and the results will be striking. The blocks are all a type of square called a Triangle Square, which is a square made up of two different-colored triangles.

Sometimes a Zigzag quilt is called "Streak of Lightning" because the early quilt-makers saw the resemblance between a completed Zigzag quilt and a lightning bolt across the prairie sky.

See page 147 for Triangle Square techniques.

Streaks of Color

Approximate Size: 48" x 48"

Materials

1/4 yard yellow
3/8 yard dark blue
3/8 yard green
5/8 yard medium blue
3/8 yard red
1 1/4 yards black
1/2 yard black (first border)
5/8 yard binding
3 yards backing
Batting

Cutting
Squares

10 squares, 3 7/8", yellow
12 squares, 3 7/8", dark blue
20 squares, 3 7/8", green
36 squares, 3 7/8", medium blue
20 squares, 3 7/8", red
98 squares, 3 7/8", black

Finishing

6 strips, 3 1/2"-wide, black (border)
6 strips, 2 1/2"-wide, binding

Instructions

TRIANGLE SQUARES

1. Draw a line diagonally from corner to corner on wrong side of colored squares. (**Diagram 1**)

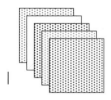

2. Place a colored square right sides together with a black square; sew 1/4" from both sides of drawn line. (**Diagram 2**)

3. Cut along drawn line for two triangle squares. (**Diagram 3**)

4. Repeat for all colored and black squares. (**Diagram 4**)

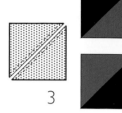

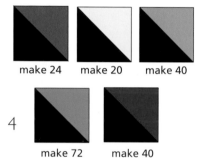

make 24   make 20   make 40

make 72   make 40

FINISHING

1. For first section, place triangle squares in seven rows of seven referring to **Diagram 5**. Sew together in rows then sew rows together. Repeat for three more sections.

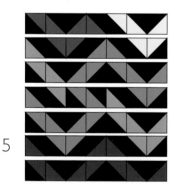

6

2. Sew two sections together giving one a quarter turn. (**Diagram 6**) Repeat.

3. Sew halves together being sure to turn the lower half. (**Diagram 7**)

4. Measure quilt top lengthwise. Sew and cut 3¹/₂"-wide black strips to that length; repeat. Sew to sides of quilt.

5. Measure quilt crosswise. Sew and cut 3¹/₂"-wide black strips to that length; repeat. Sew to top and bottom of quilt top.

6. Refer to Finishing Your Quilt, pages 152-153, to complete your quilt.

7

Streaks of Color Quilt Layout

Appliqué   Borders   English Paper Piecing   Foundation Piecing
Kaleidoscope Quilts   Postage Stamp Quilting   Redwork
Rotary Cutting   Sashiko   Stitch and Flip
Strip Piecing   Templates   Watercolor Quilts   Yo-Yo's
Finishing Your Quilt

Techniques

BEFORE YOU BEGIN—A WORD ABOUT FABRIC

For over a hundred years, quilts have been made with 100% cotton fabric, and this remains today the fabric of choice for most quilters.

There are many properties in cotton that make it especially well suited to quiltmaking. There is less distortion in cotton fabric, thereby affording the quilter greater security in making certain that even the smallest bits of fabric will fit together. Because a quilt block made of cotton can be ironed flat with a steam iron, a puckered area, created by mistake, can be fixed. The sewing machine needle can move through cotton with a great deal of ease when compared to some synthetic fabrics. While you may find that quilt artists today often use other kinds of fabric to create the quilts quickly and accurately, 100% cotton is strongly recommended.

Cotton fabric today is produced in so many wonderful and exciting combinations of prints and solids that it is often difficult to pick colors for your quilt. We've chosen our favorite colors for these quilts, but don't be afraid to make your own choices

For years, quilters were advised to prewash all of their fabric to test for colorfastness and shrinkage. Now most quilters don't bother to prewash all of their fabric but they do pretest. Cut a strip about 2" wide from each piece of fabric that you will use in your quilt. Measure both the length and the width of the strip. Then immerse it in a bowl of very hot water, using a separate bowl for each piece of fabric. Be especially concerned about reds and dark blues because they have a tendency to bleed if the initial dyeing was not done properly. If it's one of your favorite fabrics that's bleeding, you might be able to salvage the fabric.

Try washing the fabric in very hot water until you've washed out all of the excess dye. Unfortunately, fabrics that continue to bleed after they have been washed repeatedly will bleed forever. So eliminate them right at the start.

Now, take each one of the strips and iron them dry with a hot iron. Be especially careful not to stretch the strip. When the strips are completely dry, measure and compare them to the size of your original strip. If all of your fabric is shrinking the same amount, you don't have to worry about uneven shrinkage in your quilt. When you wash the final quilt, the puckering that will result may give you the look of an antique quilt. If you don't want this look, you are going to have to wash and dry all of your fabric before you start cutting. Iron the fabric using some spray starch or sizing to give the fabric a crisp finish.

If you are never planning to wash your quilt, i.e. your quilt is intended to be a wall hanging, you could eliminate the pre-testing process. You may run the risk, however, of some future relative to whom you have willed your quilts deciding that the wall hanging needs freshening by washing.

Before beginning to work, make sure that your fabric is absolutely square. If it is not, you will have difficulty cutting square pieces. Fabric is woven with crosswise and lengthwise threads. Lengthwise threads should be parallel to the selvage (that's the finished edge along the sides; sometimes the fabric company prints its name along the selvage), and crosswise threads should be perpendicular to the selvage. If fabric is off grain, you can usually straighten it by pulling gently on the true bias in the opposite direction to the off-grain edge. Continue doing this until the crosswise threads are at a right angle to the lengthwise threads.

APPLIQUÉ

Hand Appliqué

Supplies

For hand appliqué there are a few basic supplies that you will need— many of which will most likely be found in your sewing basket.

Needles: Use a needle that is comfortable for you to work with. It can be a *sharp*—general use needle, a *between*—used mainly for hand quilting or even a *straw* needle—extra fine sewing needle. As long as it is sharp and easy for you to handle, it will work for appliqué.

Thread: Use 100 percent cotton thread that matches the color of the piece you are appliquéing. A thin-weight thread such as #60 is recommended.

Pins: Use thin, sharp pins that are short in length to help keep your thread from getting tangled.

Freezer paper: Use freezer paper— found in most grocery stores—for the templates for your appliqué.

Thimble: Use a well-fitted thimble when you appliqué.

Iron: Use an iron to press seam allowances onto freezer paper. The small craft irons available today are wonderful to use.

Technique

Trace pattern pieces onto the dull side of freezer paper. Be sure to trace each piece the number of times that pattern will be used in your project. Cut freezer paper along drawn lines. (**Diagram 1**)

1

Place freezer paper pattern shiny side up onto wrong side of fabric. Cut out fabric about 1/4" from the edge of the freezer paper. (**Diagram 2**)

2

Clip seam allowances along inside curves. Never clip outside curves. (**Diagram 3**)

3

Using a hot iron, press seam allowance onto freezer paper. The heat of the iron will cause the shiny side of freezer paper to adhere temporarily to the fabric. (**Diagram 4**)

4

Prepare all appliqué pieces in the same manner. Do not remove freezer paper.

Cut background fabric the size specified in the project directions; press. For placement guides, fold background in half, then in quarters. (**Diagram 5**)

5

Place background on a flat ironing surface. Using the photograph and/or placement guide, position the first piece on background fabric. Continue placing appliqué pieces until a pleasing arrangement is achieved. (**Diagram 6**)

6

Iron pieces in place, then baste or pin. **Note:** *Ironing pieces will only provide a temporary hold, therefore pinning or basting is necessary.*

Stitch edges of appliqués using matching thread and an invisible stitch. (**Diagram 7**)

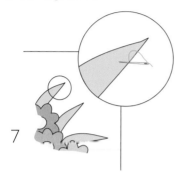

7

When all pieces are appliquéd in place, carefully make slits in the background fabric and remove freezer paper. Cut away fabric about 1/4" from stitching lines. (**Diagram 8**)

8

Two-Layer Designs

Some appliqué pieces such as the flowers in Spring Basket, page 10, are made up of two layers. It is best to appliqué the top layer onto the bottom first before appliquéing to background

fabric. Place the top (center) piece onto the Petal piece and appliqué in place. Turn Petal piece over, make a small slit and remove freezer paper and trim backing $1/4$" from stitching. (**Diagram 9**)

Fusible Appliqué

There are many different paper-backed fusible products on the market today. Each has its own unique characteristics that will help you decide which to use when making a quilt. Always be sure to follow the manufacturer's directions as each product differs greatly.

The Honolulu Fantasy quilt, page 42, uses a lightweight paper-backed fusible web such as Lite Steam a Seam® by The Warm™ Company. This will enable you to use a machine zigzag to appliqué the edges. Using a heavyweight brand will cause your needle to gum up and possibly break.

Trace the patterns onto the paper side of the fusible web following the manufacturer's directions. Be especially careful because pattern pieces that are not symmetrical will end up as mirror images of the finished project. Cut out the pattern pieces from the fusible web.

Now position fusible web pattern with paper side up onto wrong side of fabric; fuse in place with hot iron. **Note:** *Refer to manufacturer's directions for heating setting and pressing time for the product you are using.*

Machine Appliqué

Using a machine Zigzag or Blanket stitch and matching or invisible thread, stitch along all raw edges of appliqué. You may want to practice on another piece of fabric to see which zigzag width and length works best for you.

BORDERS

Borders are usually added to the top, sides and bottom of a quilt.

Simple Borders

Step 1: To add your borders, measure the quilt top lengthwise and cut two border strips to that length by the width measurement given in the instructions. Strips may have to be pieced to achieve the correct length.

Step 2: To make the joining seam less noticeable, sew the strips together diagonally. Place two strips right sides together at right angles. Sew a diagonal seam. (**Diagram 10**)

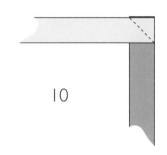

Step 3: Trim excess fabric $1/4$" from stitching. (**Diagram 11**)

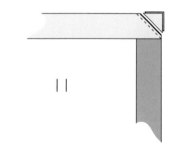

Step 4: Press seam open. (**Diagram 12**)

Step 5: Sew strips to the sides of the quilt.

Step 6: Now measure the quilt top crosswise, being sure to include the borders you have just added. Cut two border strips to that length, following the width measurement given in the instructions.

Step 7: Add these borders to the top and bottom of the quilt.

Step 8: Repeat this process for any additional borders. Use the $1/4$" seam allowance at all times and press all of the seams toward the border just added. Press the quilt top carefully.

Mitered Borders

Mitered borders are much more time-consuming than simple borders, but the results may well be worth the effort.

Step 1: Measure the quilt top lengthwise. Cut two strips that length plus twice the finished border width plus $1/2$" for seam allowances (piece if necessary to achieve the length needed).

Step 2: Measure the quilt top crosswise. Cut, piecing if necessary, two strips that length plus twice the finished border width plus $1/2$".

Step 3: Find the midpoint of one of the side border strips by folding strip in half. (**Diagram 13**)

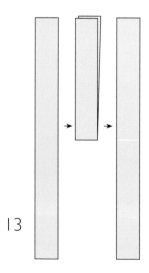

Step 4: Place strip right sides together with quilt top matching midpoint of border with midpoint of quilt side. Pin in place. (**Diagram 14**)

Step 5: Pin border to quilt top along entire side. The border strip will extend beyond the quilt top at both ends.

Step 6: Beginning ¼" from top edge of quilt top, sew border strip to quilt top, ending ¼" from bottom edge. Backstitch at beginning and ending of sewing. (**Diagram 15**) Repeat with remaining border strips being careful not to catch extended border strips edges in your sewing.

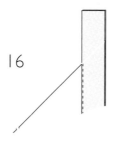

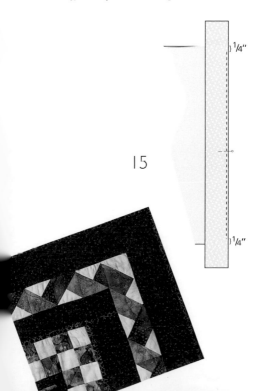

Step 7: To finish corners fold quilt top in half diagonally; borders will extend straight up and away from quilt.

Step 8: Place ruler along folded edge of quilt top going into border strip; draw a diagonal line on the border. (**Diagram 16**)

Step 9: Beginning at corner of quilt top, stitch along drawn line to edge of border strip (**Diagram 17**)

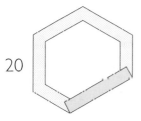

Step 10: Open quilt at corner to check miter. If satisfied, trim excess fabric ¼" from diagonal seam. (**Diagram 18**)

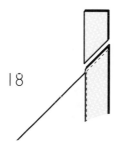

Repeat process at remaining three corners.

ENGLISH PAPER PIECING

Note: *Precut hexagon shapes can be purchased or you can trace the shape several times onto paper or use a copier to make the needed number of hexagons for your project.*

Step 1: Glue a paper hexagon onto wrong side of a fabric hexagon using a dab of glue from a fabric glue stick. (**Diagram 19**)

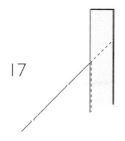

Step 2: Fold over one straight edge of fabric hexagon onto paper hexagon; glue in place with a dab of glue stick. (**Diagram 20**)

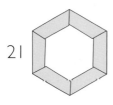

Step 3: Continue gluing raw edges of fabric hexagon onto paper. (**Diagram 21**)

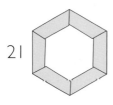

Step 4: Repeat step 3 with all fabric and paper hexagons needed for your project.

Step 5: Place the first two hexagons right sides together. Thread a sharp needle and knot one end. Beginning at corner of hexagon, whipstitch pieces together using matching thread and short stitches. Pick up only one or two threads on each hexagon and your stitches will be practically invisible on the right side of the hexagons. Continue whip-stitching to opposite corner. (**Diagram 22**)

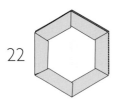

22

Step 6: Take a couple of extra stitches in corner then insert needle through fold of top hexagon and pass needle under folded edge to corner where stitching began. (**Diagram 23**)

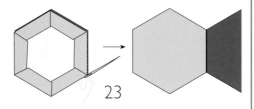

23

Step 7: Open sewn hexagons flat. Sew next hexagon in same manner following steps 5 and 6. (**Diagram 24**)

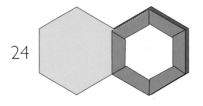

24

Step 8: Continue sewing hexagons around center hexagon, taking a couple stitches at each corner until block is complete. (**Diagram 25**)

25

FOUNDATION PIECING

Materials

Before you begin, decide the kind of foundation on which you are planning to piece the blocks.

Paper

The most popular choice is paper. It's readily available and fairly inexpensive. You can use copy paper, newsprint, tracing paper—even computer paper. The paper does not remain a permanent part of your quilt as it is removed once the blocks are completely sewn.

Fabric

If you choose to hand piece your block, you may want to choose fabric as your foundation. Just remember that fabric is not removed after you make your block so you will have another layer to quilt through. This may be a problem if you are planning to hand quilt. Using fabric might be an advantage, however, if you want to use some non-traditional quilting fabrics, such as satin, since the fabric foundation will add stability to the block. Fabric makes a good choice for crazy quilts. If you do decide to use fabric, choose a lightweight and light-colored fabric, such as muslin, that will allow you to see through for ease in tracing.

Other Materials

Another option for foundation materials is Tear Away™ or Fun-dation™, translucent non-woven materials combining both the advantages of both paper and fabric. They are easy to see through, but like paper they can be removed with ease.

Currently a new kind of foundation material has appeared in the market place: a foundation paper that dissolves in water after use. Two companies, W.H. Collins and EZ

Quilting by Wrights are producing this product.

Preparing the Foundation

Place your foundation material over your chosen block and trace the block pattern. Use a ruler and a fine-line pencil or permanent marker, and make sure that all lines are straight. Sometimes short dashed lines or even dotted lines are easier to make. Be sure to copy all numbers. You will need to make a foundation for each block you are planning to use.

If you have a home copier, you can copy your tracing on the copy machine. Since the copy machine might slightly alter the measurements of the block, make certain that you copy each block from the original pattern.

You can also scan the block if you have a home scanner and then print out the required number of blocks.

Cutting the Fabric

In foundation piecing, you do not have to cut perfect shapes!

You can, therefore, use odd pieces of fabric: squares, strips, and rectangles. The one thing you must remember, however, is that every piece must be at least $1/4$" larger on all sides than the space it is going to cover. Strips and squares are easy: just measure the length and width of the needed space and add $1/2$" all around. Cut your strip to that measurement. Triangles, however, can be a bit tricky. In that case, measure the widest point of the triangle and cut your fabric about $1/2$" to 1" wider.

Other Supplies for Foundation Piecing

Piecing by Hand

You will need a reasonably thin needle such as a Sharp Size 10, a good quality neutral-colored thread such as size 50 cotton, some pins, a glue stick, fabric scissors, muslin or fabric for the bases.

Piecing by Machine

You will need a cleaned and oiled sewing machine, glue stick, pins, paper scissors, fabric scissors, foundation material.

Before beginning to sew your actual block by machine, determine the proper stitch length. Use a piece of the paper you are planning to use for the foundation and draw a straight line on it. Set your machine so that it sews with a fairly short stitch (about 20 stitches per inch). Sew along the line. If you can tear the paper apart with ease, you are sewing with the right length. You don't want to sew with such a short stitch that the paper falls apart by itself. If you are going to use a fabric foundation with the sewing machine, use the stitch length you normally use.

Using a Pattern

The numbers on the block show the order in which the pieces are to be placed and sewn on the base. It is extremely important that you follow the numbers; otherwise the entire process won't work.

Making the Block

The important thing to remember about making a foundation block is that the fabric pieces go on the unmarked side of the foundation while you sew on the printed side. The finished blocks are a mirror image of the original pattern.

Step 1: Hold the foundation up to a light source—even a window pane—with the unmarked side facing. Find the space marked 1 on the unmarked side and put a dab of glue there. Place the fabric right side up on the unmarked side on Space 1, making certain that the fabric overlaps at least 1/4" on all sides of space 1. (**Diagram 26**)

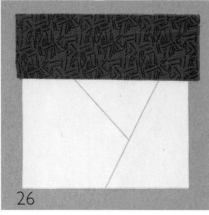

Step 2: Fold the foundation along the line between Space 1 and Space 2. Cut the fabric so that it is 1/4" from the fold. (**Diagram 27**)

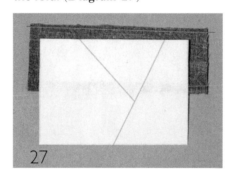

Step 3: With right sides together, place Fabric Piece 2 on Fabric Piece 1, making sure that the edge of Piece 2 is even with the just-trimmed edge of Piece 1. (**Diagram 28**)

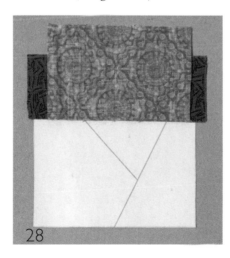

Step 4: To make certain that Piece 2 will cover Space 2, fold the fabric piece back along the line between Space 1 and Space 2. (**Diagram 29**)

Step 5: With the marked side of the foundation facing up, place the piece on the sewing machine (or sew by hand), holding both Piece 1 and Piece 2 in place. Sew along the line between Space 1 and Space 2. (**Diagram 30**)

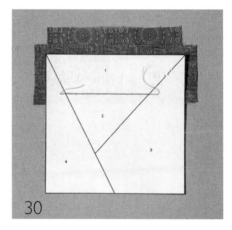

Hint: *If you use a small stitch, it will be easier to remove the paper later. Start stitching about two or three stitches before the beginning of the line and end your sewing two or three stitches beyond the line, allowing the stitches to be held in place by the next round of stitching rather than by backstitching.*

Step 6: Turn the work over and open Piece 2. Finger press the seam open. (**Diagram 31**)

Step 7: Turning the work so that the marked side is on top, fold the foundation forward along the line between Space 1+2 and Space 3. Trim about $\frac{1}{8}$" to $\frac{1}{4}$" from the fold.

It is easier to trim the paper if you pull the paper away from the stitching. If you use fabric as your foundation, fold the fabric forward as far as it will go and then start to trim. (**Diagram 32**)

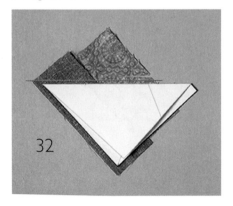

Step 8: Place Fabric #3 right side down even with the just-trimmed edge. (**Diagram 33**)

Step 9: Turn the block over to the marked side and sew along the line between Space 1+2 and Space 3. (**Diagram 34**)

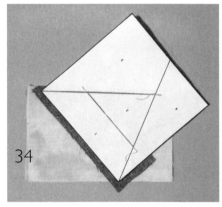

Step 10: Turn the work over, open Piece 3 and finger press the seam. (**Diagram 35**)

Step 11: In the same way you have added the other pieces, add Piece #4 to complete this block. Trim the fabric $\frac{1}{4}$" from the edge of the foundation. The foundation-pieced block is completed. (**Diagram 36**)

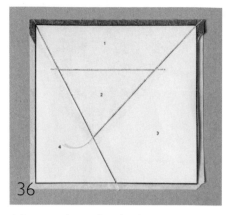

After you have finished sewing a block, don't immediately remove the paper. Since you are often piecing with tiny bits of fabric, grainline is not a factor. Therefore, some of the pieces may have been cut on the bias and may have a tendency to stretch. You can eliminate any problem with distortion by keeping the paper in place until all of the blocks have been sewn together. If, however, you want to remove the paper, stay stitch along the outer edge of the block to help keep the block in shape.

Sewing Multiple Sections

Many of the blocks in foundation piecing are created with two or more sections. These sections, which are indicated by letters, are individually pieced and then sewn together. The cutting line for these sections is indicated by a bold line. Before you start to make any of these multi-section blocks, begin by cutting the foundation piece apart so that each section is worked independently. Leave a $\frac{1}{4}$" seam allowance around each section.

Step 1: Following the instructions above for Making the Block, complete each section. Then place the sections right side together. Pin the corners of the top section to the corners of the bottom section. (**Diagram 37**)

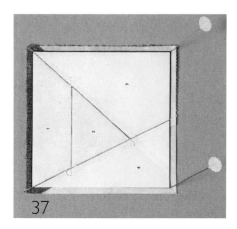
37

Step 2: If you are certain that the pieces are aligned correctly, sew the two sections together using the regular stitch length on the sewing machine. (**Diagram 38**)

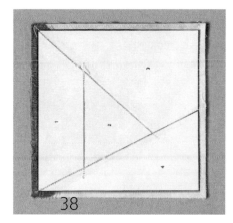
38

Step 3: Press the sections open and continue sewing the sections in pairs. (**Diagram 39**)

39

Step 4: Sew necessary pairs of sections together to complete the block. (**Diagram 40**)

40

The blocks are now ready to sew into your quilt.

What You Don't Want to Forget

1. If you plan to sew by hand, begin by taking some backstitches that will anchor the thread at the beginning of the line. Then use a backstitch every four of five stitches. End the stitching with a few backstitches.

2. If you plan to sew by machine, start stitching two or three stitches before the start of the stitching line and finish your stitching two or three stitches beyond the end.

3. Use a short stitch (about 20 stitches per inch) for paper foundations to make it easier to remove the paper. If the paper falls apart as you sew, your stitches are too short.

4. Finger press (or use an iron) each seam as you finish it.

5. Stitching which goes from a space into another space will not interfere with adding additional fabric pieces.

6. Remember to trim all seam allowances at least $1/4$".

7. When sewing points, start from the wide end and sew towards the point.

8. Unless you plan to use it only once in the block, it is a good idea to stay away from directional prints in foundation piecing.

9. When cutting pieces for foundation piecing, never worry about the grainline.

10. Always remember to sew on the marked side, placing the fabric on the unmarked side.

11. Follow the numerical order, or it won't work.

12. Once you have finished making a block do not remove the paper until the entire quilt has been finished unless you stay stitch around the outside of the block.

13. Be sure that the ink you use to make your foundation is permanent and will not wash out into your fabric.

KALEIDOSCOPE QUILTS

Start a kaleidoscope by finding colorful fabric with a lot going on. For example, choose a floral with several different colors and a variety of flower sizes.

Step 1: Cut the fabric in half lengthwise. Work with one half of the fabric to start. Find the pattern repeat and cut fabric in repeat strips. For example, if the pattern repeat is 12", cut fabric in 12" strips, cutting the number of repeats for the number of shapes you will need per block. For example, if your block needs eight repeats like in the Fanciful Twirls quilt, page 58, you will need to cut eight repeats.

Step 2: Place cut repeats exactly on top of each other. Pin or baste in place making sure the individual strips don't shift. **Hint:** *If using pins, use the flat flower head pins found in your local quilt shop. You will then be able to use your acrylic ruler and rotary cutter to cut the shapes needed for your quilt.*

Step 3: Cut the repeats in strips as specified in the pattern directions, then cut the number of shapes needed for your project.

POSTAGE STAMP QUILTMAKING

To create postage stamp quilts, you will need fusible gridded interfacing with 1" squares, available from various companies including "Quilter's Grid™"by Freudenberg Nonwovens for Pellon and "Quilt Top Express™" by June Tailor.

Step 1: Using a rotary cutter (see page 146), cut fabric in 1" strips, then cut 1" squares. You will get about 40 to 44 squares per strip.

Step 2: Place the gridded interfacing on a flat surface, bumpy side up.

Step 3: Following the block chart (see the charts for Petite Sampler, page 86), place the fabric squares in position right side up and iron down.

Step 4: Fold first vertical row onto second row with rights sides together. Join the rows with a ¼" seam allowance. (**Diagram 41**)

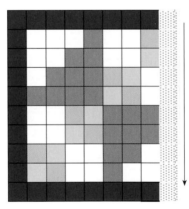

41

Step 5: Continue sewing rows alternating directions with each row. (**Diagram 42**) This will help to keep the block from getting out of shape.

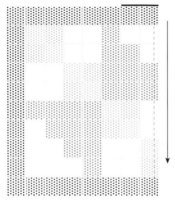

42

Step 6: Snip seams where squares butt up against each other. (**Diagram 43**) This will allow alternating seams in adjoining rows for easier sewing.

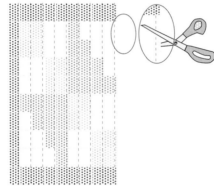

43

Step 7: Join horizontal rows together to complete block, changing direction of each row.

REDWORK

Materials

Fabric

Traditionally, the preferred background fabric would be an unbleached muslin for the embroidery; however any white or off-white 100% cotton can be used.

Needles

While there are many needles that can be used for redwork, the best to use are embroidery needles sizes 8 and 7. These are recommended because the eye of the needle is elongated, making it easier for threading.

Embroidery Floss

Use two strands of any good quality six strand embroidery floss in 18" lengths. Choose a color of red such as DMC #498 or Anchor #45.

Embroidery Hoops

You will achieve the best results if you use an embroidery hoop that will hold the project taut while you are stitching. Make certain that the hoop is larger than the pattern.

Instructions

Step 1: Cut bckground fabric into size specified in the instructions.

Step 2: Place fabric over the design and trace with a sharp lead pencil or a marking pen. Make certain that any marking material you use will disappear. Follow the manufacturer's instructions.

Step 3: Thread the floss into the needle and begin stitching by coming up from the wrong side of the fabric, leaving a 1" tail which you can secure with the first few stitches. Never use knots!

Step 4: Use the Stem Stitch to cover all traced lines. (**Diagram 44**)

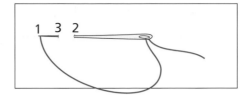
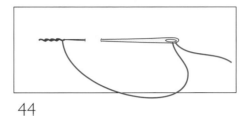

44

Step 5. Never carry the thread across the back over more than 1" and never carry the thread across an unworked area.

Step 6: When you are finished working, weave the thread through some of the stitches on the back.

ROTARY CUTTING

Supplies for Rotary Cutting

For rotary cutting, you will need three important tools: a rotary cutter, a mat and an acrylic ruler. There are currently on the market many different brands and types. Choose the kinds that you feel will work for you. Ask your quilting friends what their preferences are; then make your decision.

There are several different rotary cutters now available with special features that you might prefer such as the type of handle, whether the cutter can be used for both right- and left-handed quilters, safety features, size, and finally the cost.

Don't attempt to use the rotary cutter without an accompanying protective mat. The mat will not only protect your table from becoming scratched, but it will protect your cutter as well. The mat is self-healing and will not dull the cutting blades. Mats are available in many sizes, but if this is your first attempt at rotary cutting, an 18" x 24" mat is probably your best choice. When you are not using your mat, be sure to store it on a flat surface. Otherwise your mat will bend. If you want to keep your mat from warping, make certain that it is not sitting in direct sunlight; the heat can cause the mat to warp. You will not be able to cut accurately when you use a bent or warped mat.

Another must for cutting accurate strips is a strong straight edge. Acrylic rulers are the perfect choice for this. There are many different brands of acrylic rulers on the market, and they come in several widths and lengths. Either a 6" x 24" or a 6" x 12" ruler will be the most useful. The longer ruler will allow you to fold your fabric only once while the smaller size will require folding the fabric twice. Make sure that your ruler has 1/8" increment markings in both directions plus a 45-degree marking.

Cutting Strips With a Rotary Cutter

Before beginning to work, iron your fabric to remove the wrinkles. Fold the fabric in half, lengthwise, bringing the selvage edges together. Fold in half again. Make sure that there are no wrinkles in the fabric.

Now place the folded fabric on the cutting mat. Place the fabric length on the right side if you are right-handed (A) or on the left side if you are left-handed (B). The fold of the fabric should line up along one of the grid lines printed on the mat. (**Diagram 45**)

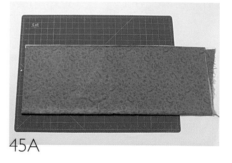

45A

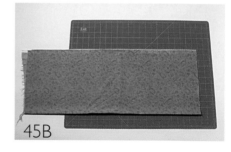

45B

Straighten one of the cut edges first. Lay the acrylic ruler on the mat near the cut edge; the ruler markings should be even with the grid on the mat. Hold the ruler firmly with your left hand (or, with your right hand if your are left-handed). To provide extra stability, keep your small finger off the mat. Now hold the rotary cutter with blade against the ruler and cut away from you in one quick motion. (**Diagram 46**)

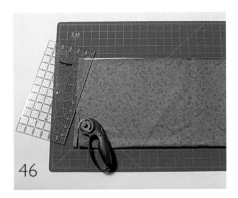

46

Place the ruler on the required width line along the cut edge of the fabric and cut the strip, making sure that you always cut away from you—never toward you. Cut the number of strips called for in the directions. (**Diagram 47**)

47

After you have cut a few strips, you will want to check to make certain that your fabric continues to be perfectly square. To do this, just line up the crosswise markings along the folded edge of fabric and the lengthwise edge of the ruler next to the end of fabric you are cutting. Cut off uneven edge. If you fail to do this, your strips may be bowed with a "v" in the center, causing your piecing to become inaccurate as you continue working.

Cutting Squares and Rectangles

Now that you have cut your strips, you can begin to cut squares or rectangles. Place a stack of strips on the cutting mat. You will be more successful in cutting—at least in the beginning—if you work with no more than four strips at a time. Make certain that the strips are lined up very evenly. Following the instructions given for the quilt, cut the required number of squares or rectangles. (**Diagram 48**)

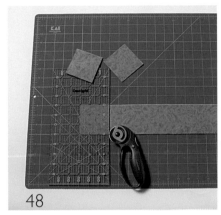

48

Cutting Triangles

Once your squares are cut, you can cut triangles, including Half-Square Triangles, Quarter-Square Triangles and Triangle Squares.

Half-Square Triangles

The short sides of a Half-Square Triangle are on the short grain of the fabric. This is especially necessary if the short edges are on the outer side of the block.

Cut the squares the size indicated in the instructions, then cut the square in half diagonally. (**Diagram 49**)

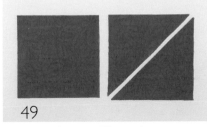

49

Quarter-Square Triangles

These are used when the long edge of the triangle must be on the straight grain. This is important when the long edge is on the outside edge of the block. Again, cut the squares

the proper size; then cut diagonally into quarters. (**Diagram 50**)

Triangle Squares

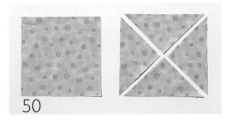

50

These are squares made up of two different-colored triangles. To make these squares, you can cut individual triangles as described in Half-Square Triangles. Then sew two triangles together. A quick method, especially if you have several triangle squares with the same fabric, is to sew two squares together. First draw a diagonal line on the wrong side of the lighter square. Place two squares right sides together and sew $1/4$" from each side of the drawn line.

Cut along the drawn line, and you have created two Triangle Squares. (**Diagram 51**)

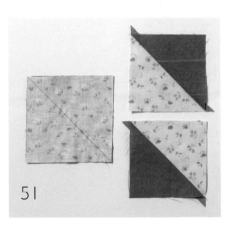

51

SASHIKO

Step 1: Mark the quilting pattern on the quilt top. Since the fabric is dark, you will need to use a white pencil, dressmaker's carbon or transfer paper. Place carbon or transfer paper right side down on quilt top. Place quilting design on top of transfer paper. Trace over quilting design with a pointed tool such as a knitting needle or ballpoint pen until entire design is traced.

Step 2: Layer the quilt top with batting and backing.

Step 3: Place quilt in a quilting hoop, not an embroidery hoop. The tension should not be too tight.

Step 4: Thread a "between" needle with one strand of white hand quilting thread. Use the size needle that is most comfortable for you. Between needles are shorter than regular needles, but they are sharp and strong. The larger the needle size the shorter the needle.

Step 5: Make a knot on one end of the thread. Starting on the quilt top, pass the needle through the top and batting layers; bring needle back through the surface of the quilt top where you will begin quilting. Tug the needle until the knot pops through the top layer and is hidden within the batting layer.

Step 6: Begin taking short running stitches using a rocking motion. Start needle in a vertical position and place as many stitches as you are comfortable with on the needle before bringing the needle through. Try to bring needle to a vertical position with the start of each stitch.

Step 7: When you come to the end of your thread, you must again bury the knot within the batting layer. Keeping the needle threaded, wrap the thread twice around the needle. Pull the needle and tighten the knot.

Note: *The knot should be slightly above the quilt top, about 1/4" away. Insert the needle back into the hole made by the last stitch and go through the batting layer for about 1/2" to 1" away. Come up through the quilt top. Pull until the knot is against the quilt top and tug needle until the knot is inside the batting layer. Cut the thread end.*

STITCH AND FLIP

This is a method for quickly creating triangles and octagons or trapezoids.

Instead of cutting these shapes, you cut and sew squares or triangles together. (**Diagram 52**)

52

With right sides together, place a small square in the corner of a larger square or rectangle. Sew diagonally from corner to corner of the small square. (**Diagram 53**)

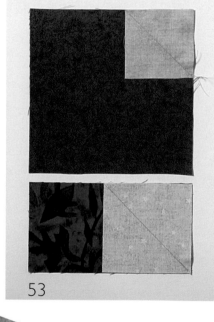

53

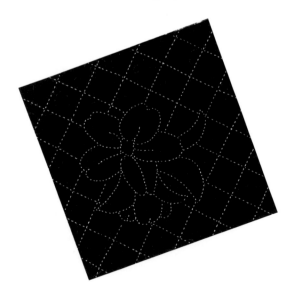

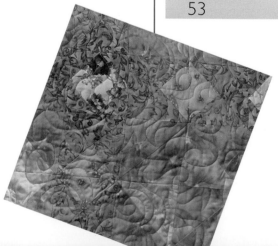

Trim the corner about 1/4" from the seam line. (**Diagram 54**)

54

Flip the triangle over and press. (**Diagram 55**)

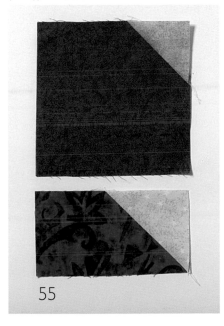

55

Repeat at the other corners. (**Diagram 56**)

56

STRIP PIECING

Strip piecing is a much faster and easier method of making quilts rather than creating the blocks piece by piece. With this method, two or more strips are sewn together and then cut at certain intervals. For instance, if a block is made up of several 3" finished squares, cut 3 1/2"-wide strips along the crosswise grain. (**Diagram 57**)

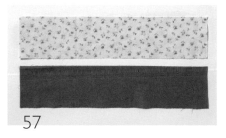

57

With right sides together, sew two strips along the length. The seam should be pressed across the dark side of the fabric. (**Diagram 58**)

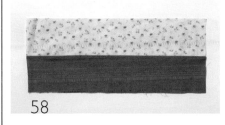

58

Cut across strips at 3 1/2" intervals to create pairs of 3 1/2" squares. (**Diagram 59**)

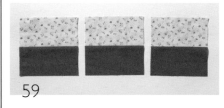

59

149

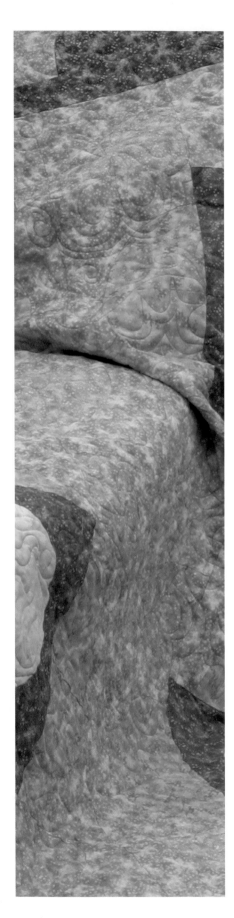

TEMPLATES

Drunkard's Path, page 104, is made using templates. Acrylic templates in the proper size are now available in many quilt stores, but if you do not have access to acrylic templates, you can easily make templates using the patterns found on page 190. These templates are designed to be used for either machine or hand piecing. If you are planning to piece your block by machine, the template should be cut on the solid line to include the $1/4''$ seam allowance. If the template is to be used for hand piecing, cut the template on the dotted line and add the $1/4''$ seam allowance when you cut the fabric (see Cutting the Pieces below).

Trace the template pattern onto tracing paper; then glue the pattern onto your choice of template material. Templates can be made out of heavy cardboard, template plastic, even sandpaper. It is important that the templates be cut out carefully because if they are not accurate, the pieces will not fit together. Use a pair of good size scissors (not the scissors that you might plan to use for cutting the fabric) a single-edged razor blade or a craft knife.

It is important to remember that the constant tracing around a cardboard or sandpaper template may cause the edges to wear so that the pattern pieces may begin to change their shape. Make certain that your template stays consistent, and be prepared to make new templates when the original ones are no longer accurate.

Cutting the Pieces

Start by laying your fabric on a smooth surface with the wrong side up. Lay the template on the wrong side of the fabric near the top left edge of the material (not on the selvage). Using a marking tool, such as a hard lead pencil or a fabric marking pen, make the proper markings. Always be sure to test all marking materials to make sure they will not run when wet before using them.

Continue moving the template and tracing it on the fabric the required number of times, moving from left to right and keeping the straight sides parallel with the grain of the fabric. If your template is for machine piecing, cut along the outside drawn line.

If your template is for hand piecing, measure $1/4''$ around the drawn line and using a ruler, draw this second line. This will be your cutting line, and the first line (where you traced the template) will be your stitching line. The seam allowance does not have to be absolutely accurate, but the stitching line must be perfect or the pieces will not fit together.

WATERCOLOR QUILTS

Watercolor quilts are made with 2" cut squares placed onto gridded fusible interfacing. Use a wide variety of fabrics with many colors and prints with motifs varying from medium to large. Try to find fabrics that have very dense patterns as well as those with motifs that are spread out. For example, in the Butterfly Garden quilt, page 116, notice the density in the floral garden area at the bottom of the quilt. The garden area flows subtly into the background by using fabrics with a similar background color (blue) and floral designs that are more spread out as they go from the garden toward the background. To keep the shape of the butterfly, use dense floral patterned fabrics with colors that contrast with the background fabric.

To create a watercolor quilt, you will need fusible gridded interfacing with 2" squares. You can also use the gridded interfacing with 1" squares but remember that you will be covering four squares of the interfacing with square of fabric.

Step 1: Using a rotary cutter (see page 146), cut fabric in 2" strips then cut 2" squares. You will get about 20 to 22 squares per strip.

Step 2: Place the gridded interfacing on a flat surface, bumpy side up.

Step 3: Following the block chart (see the charts for Butterfly Garden, page 191), place the fabric squares in position right side up and iron down.

Step 4: Fold first vertical row onto second row with right sides together. Join the rows with a ¼" seam allowance. (**Diagram 60**)

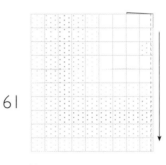

60

Step 5: Continue sewing rows alternating directions with each row. (**Diagram 61**) This will help to keep the block from getting out of shape.

61

Step 6: Snip seams where squares butt up against each other. (**Diagram 62**) This will allow alternating seams in adjoining rows for easier sewing.

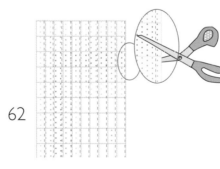

62

Step 7: Join horizontal rows together to complete block, changing the direction of each row. (**Diagram 63**)

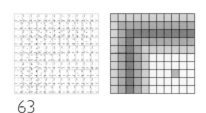

63

YO-YO'S

Cut a fabric circle that is twice the diameter of the finished Yo-Yo plus ¼" seam allowance.

Step 1: Fold edge of circle toward wrong side about ¼". (**Diagram 64**)

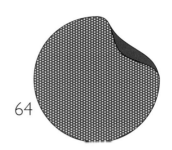

64

Step 2: Thread your sewing needle and knot one end. Using a running stitch, sew along folded edge of circle. (**Diagram 65**)

65

Step 3: Pull thread to draw up circle and knot end of thread. (**Diagram 66**)

Step 4: Flatten circle with small hole in center. (**Diagram 67**)

66   67

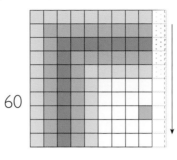

151

FINISHING YOUR QUILT

Attaching the Batting and Backing

There are a number of different types of batting on the market today including the new fusible battings that eliminate the need for basting. Your choice of batting will depend upon how you are planning to use your quilt. If the quilt is to serve as a wall hanging, you will probably want to use a thin cotton batting. A quilt made with a thin cotton or cotton/polyester blend works best for machine quilting. Very thick polyester batting should be used only for tied quilts.

The best fabric for quilt backing is 100% cotton fabric. If your quilt is larger than the available fabric you will have to piece your backing fabric. When joining the fabric, try not to have a seam going down the center. Instead cut off the selvages and make a center strip that is about 36" wide and have narrower strips at the sides. Seam the pieces together and carefully iron the seams open. (This is one of the few times in making a quilt that a seam should be pressed open.) Several fabric manufacturers are now selling fabric in 90" or 108"-widths for use as backing fabric.

It is a good idea to remove the batting from its wrapping 24 hours before you plan to use it and open it out to full size. You will find that the batting will now lie flat when you are ready to use it.

The batting and the backing should be cut about one to two inches larger on all sides than the quilt top. Place the backing wrong side up on a flat surface. Smooth out the batting on top of this, matching the outer edges. Center the quilt top, right side up, on top of the batting.

Now the quilt layers must be held together before quilting, and there are several methods for doing this:

Safety-pin Basting: Starting from the center and working toward the edges, pin through all layers at one time with large safety pins. The pins should be placed no more than 4" apart. As you work, think of your quilting plan to make sure that the pins will avoid prospective quilting lines.

Thread Basting: Baste the three layers together with long stitches. Start in the center and sew toward the edges in a number of diagonal lines.

Quilt-gun Basting: This handy trigger tool pushes nylon tags through all layers of the quilt. Start in the center and work toward the outside edges. The tags should be placed about 4" apart. You can sew right over the tags, which can then be easily removed by cutting them off with scissors.

Spray or Heat-set Basting: Several manufacturers have spray adhesives available especially for quilters. Apply these products by following the manufacturers' directions. You might want to test these products before you use them to make sure that they meet your requirements.

Fusible Iron-on Batting: These battings are a wonderful new way to hold quilt layers together without using any of the other time-consuming methods of basting. Again, you will want to test these battings to be certain that you are happy with the results. Follow the manufacturers' directions.

Quilting

If you like the process of hand quilting, you can—of course—finish these projects by hand quilting. However, if you want to finish these quilts quickly, you might want to use a sewing machine for quilting.

If you have never used a sewing machine for quilting, you may want to find a book and read about the technique. You do not need a special machine for quilting. Just make sure that your machine has been oiled and is in good working condition.

If you are going to do machine quilting, you should invest in an even-feed foot. This foot is designed to feed the top and bottom layers of a quilt evenly through the machine. The foot prevents puckers from forming as you machine quilt. Use a fine transparent nylon thread in the top and regular sewing thread in the bobbin.

Quilting in the ditch is one of the easiest ways to machine quilt. This is a term used to describe stitching along the seam line between two pieces of fabric. Using your fingers, pull the blocks or pieces apart slightly and machine stitch right between the two pieces. The stitching will look better if you keep the stitching to the side of the seam that does not have the extra bulk of the seam allowance under it. The quilting will be hidden in the seam.

Free-form machine quilting can be used to quilt around a design or to quilt a motif. The quilting is done with a darning foot and the feed dogs down on the sewing machine. It takes practice to master Free-form quilting because you are controlling the movement of the quilt under the needle rather than the sewing machine moving the quilt. You can quilt in any direction—up and down, side-to-side and even in circles—without pivoting the quilt around the needle. Practice this quilting method before trying it on your quilt.

Attaching the Continuous Machine Binding

Once the quilt has been quilted, the edges must be bound. Start by trimming the backing and batting even with the quilt top. Measure the quilt top and cut enough 2¹/₂"-wide strips to go around all four sides of the quilt plus 12". Join the strips end to end with diagonal seams and trim the corners. Press the seams open. (**Diagram 68**)

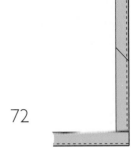

On the back of the quilt, position the binding in the middle of one side, keeping the raw edges together. Sew the binding to the quilt with the ¹/₄" seam allowance, beginning about three inches below the folded end of the binding. (**Diagram 70**)

Continue in the same way around the remaining sides of the quilt. Stop about 2" away from the starting point. Trim any excess binding and tuck it inside the folded end. Finish the stitching. (**Diagram 72**)

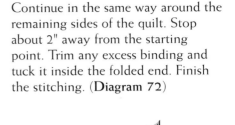

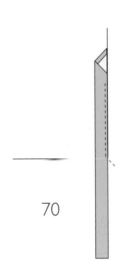

70

At the corner, stop ¹/₄" from the edge of the quilt and backstitch.

Fold binding away from quilt so it is at a right angle to edge just sewn. Then, fold the binding back on itself so the fold is on the quilt edge and the raw edges are aligned with the adjacent side of the quilt. Begin sewing at the quilt edge. (**Diagram 71**)

Fold the binding to the front of the quilt so the seam line is covered; machine-stitch the binding in place on the front of the quilt. Use a straight stitch or tiny zigzag with invisible or matching thread.
Hint: *If you have a sewing machine that does embroidery stitches, you may want to use your favorite stitch.*

Always sign and date your quilt when finished. You can make a label by cross-stitching or embroidering or even writing on a label or on the back of your quilt with a permanent marking pen. If you are friends with your computer, you can even create an attractive label on the computer.

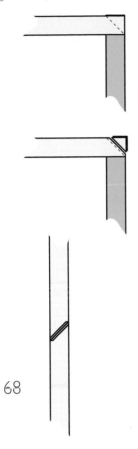

68

Cut one end of the strip at a 45-degree angle and press under ¹/₄". Press entire strip in half lengthwise, wrong sides together. (**Diagram 69**)

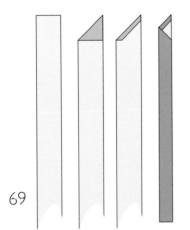

69

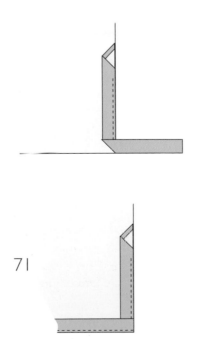

71

Appliqué   Crazy Quilt   Embroidery
Foundation Piecing   Hawaiian Quilt   Japanese Quilt
Log Cabin Quilt   Medallion   Stained Glass
Templates   Watercolor

Patterns

Patterns

SPRING BASKET APPLIQUÉ PATTERNS

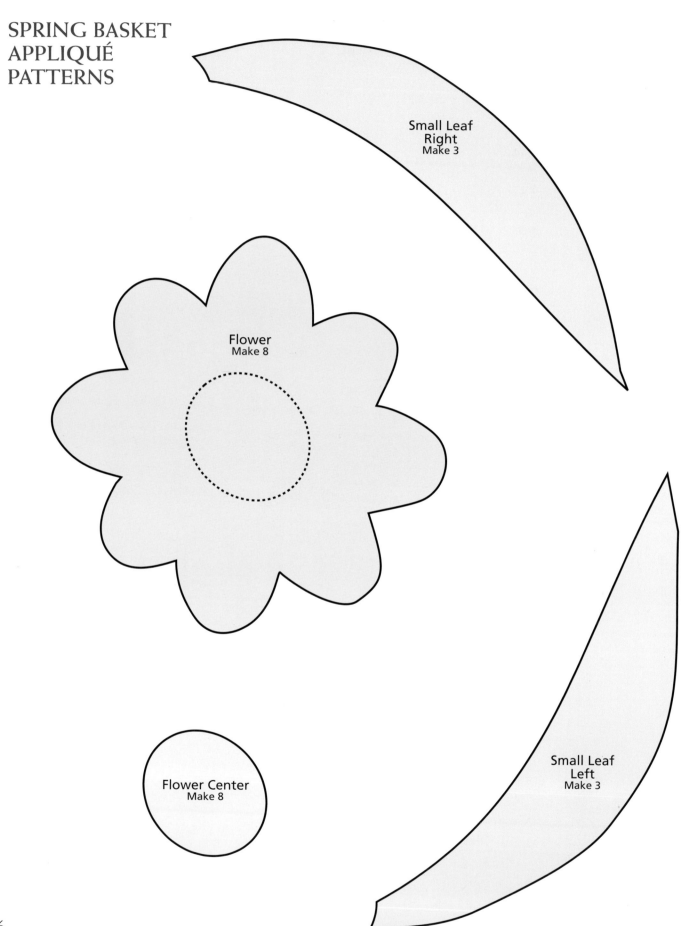

Small Leaf
Right
Make 3

Flower
Make 8

Flower Center
Make 8

Small Leaf
Left
Make 3

SPRING BASKET
APPLIQUÉ PATTERNS

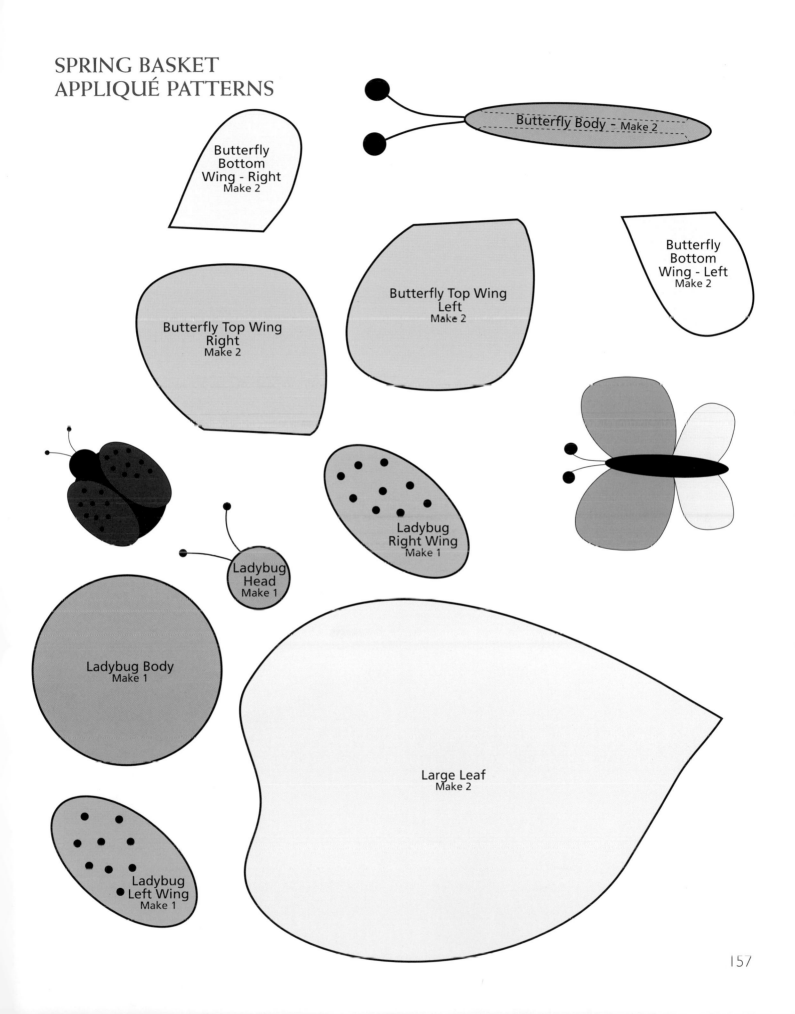

Butterfly Body - Make 2

Butterfly
Bottom
Wing - Right
Make 2

Butterfly
Bottom
Wing - Left
Make 2

Butterfly Top Wing
Right
Make 2

Butterfly Top Wing
Left
Make 2

Ladybug
Right Wing
Make 1

Ladybug
Head
Make 1

Ladybug Body
Make 1

Large Leaf
Make 2

Ladybug
Left Wing
Make 1

SPRING BASKET
APPLIQUÉ PATTERNS

$^1/_2$ Basket
Cut 1 -Trace pattern; flop pattern,
match dashed lines
and trace other half

TWISTED PATHS
FOUNDATION PATTERN

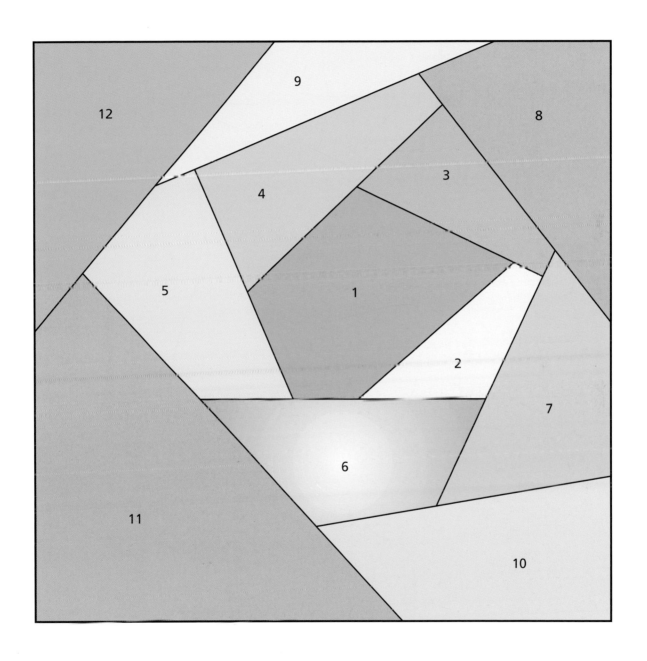

REDWORK COVERLET
EMBROIDERY PATTERN 1

REDWORK COVERLET
EMBROIDERY PATTERN 3

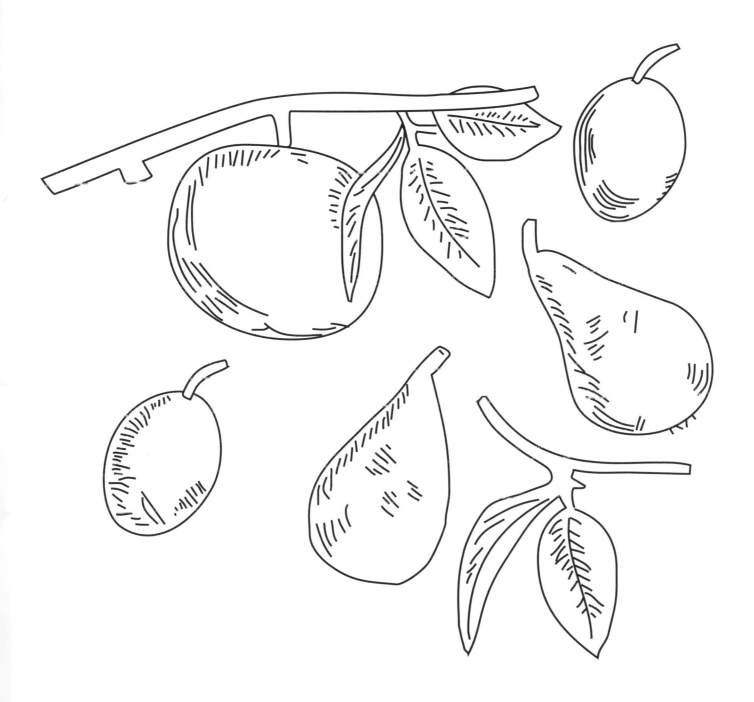

REDWORK COVERLET
EMBROIDERY PATTERN 5

REDWORK COVERLET
EMBROIDERY PATTERN 6

REDWORK COVERLET
EMBROIDERY PATTERN 7

REDWORK COVERLET
EMBROIDERY PATTERN 9

REDWORK COVERLET
EMBROIDERY PATTERN 11

REDWORK COVERLET
EMBROIDERY PATTERN 13

REDWORK COVERLET
EMBROIDERY PATTERN 15

REDWORK COVERLET
EMBROIDERY PATTERN 17

CARPENTER'S WHEEL
FOUNDATION PATTERN A

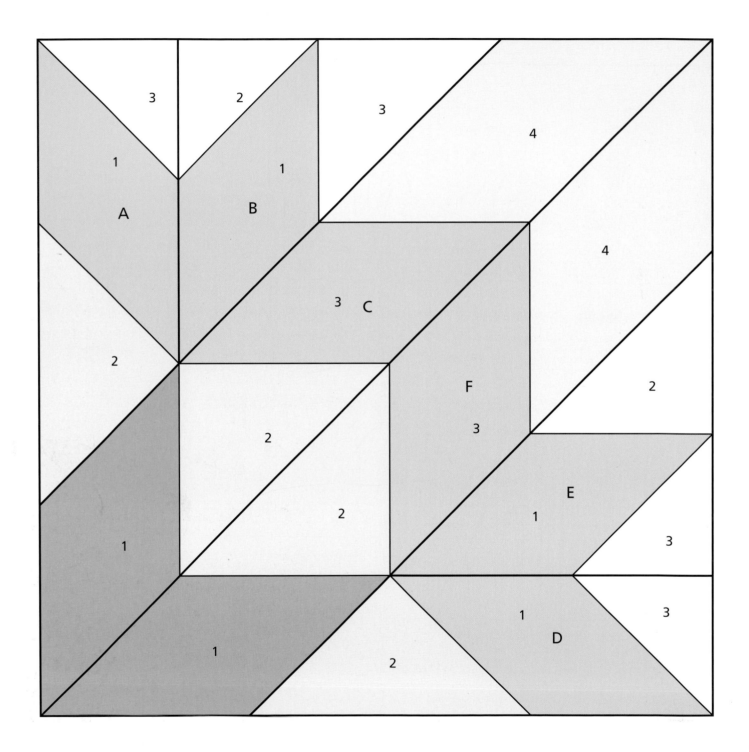

CARPENTER'S WHEEL
FOUNDATION PATTERN B

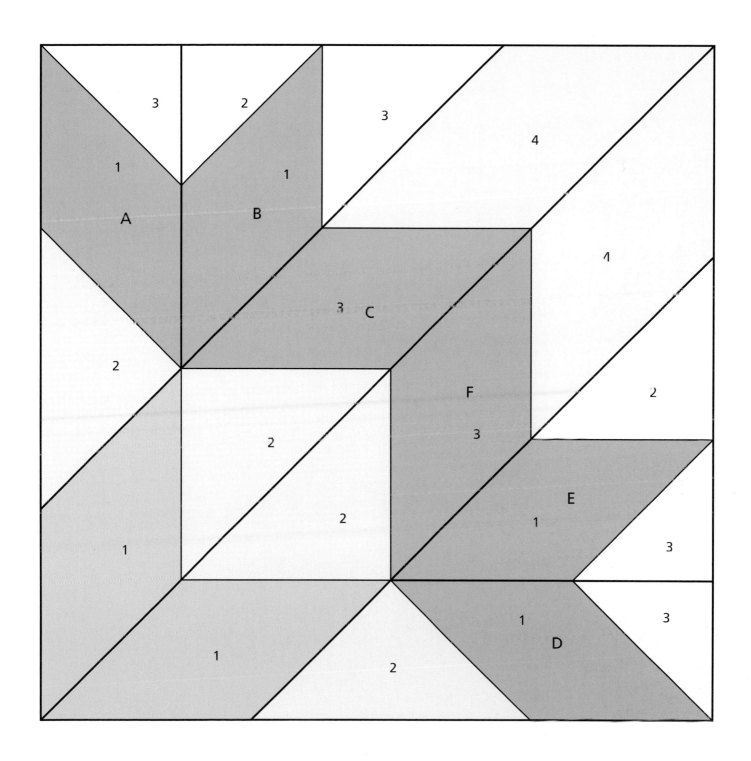

HONOLULU FANTASY
APPLIQUÉ PATTERN A

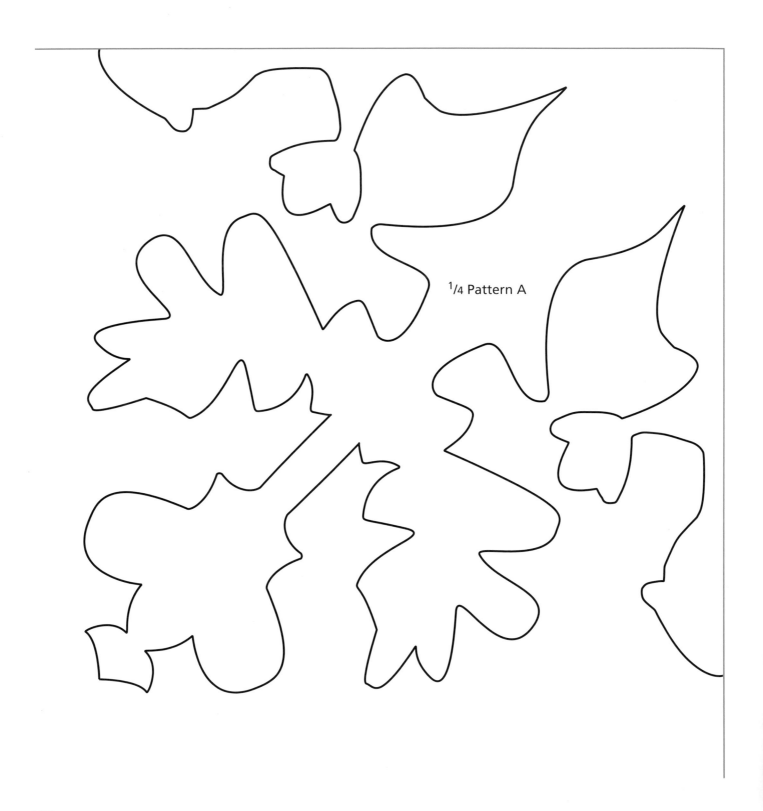

¹/4 Pattern A

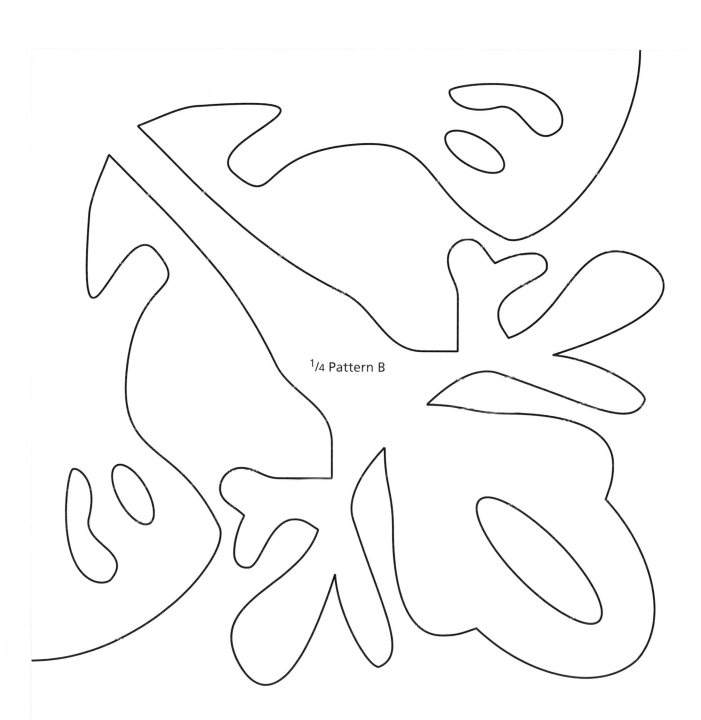

1/4 Pattern B

CHERRY BLOSSOMS
QUILTING PATTERN

CHRISTMAS IN THE CABIN
FOUNDATION PATTERN

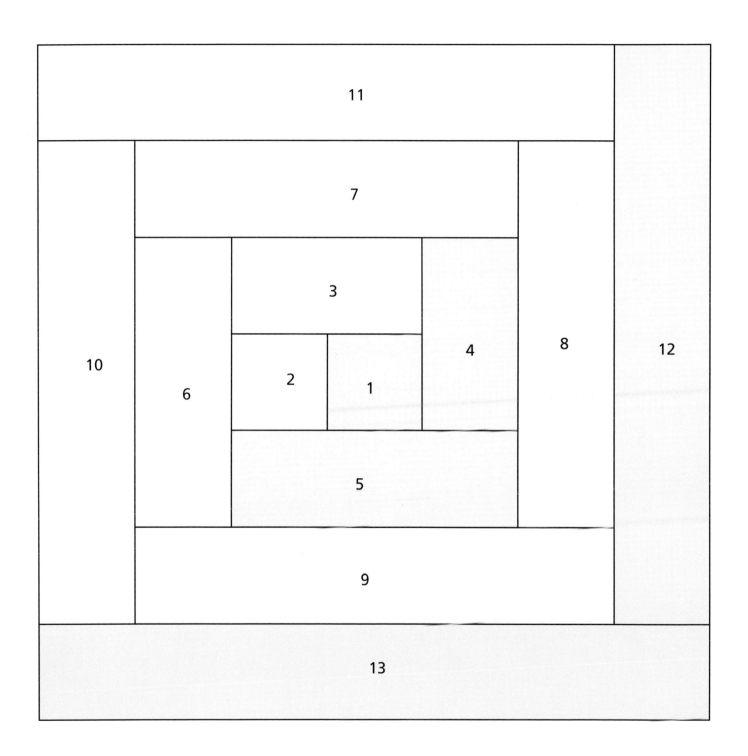

STARBURST APPLIQUÉ PATTERNS

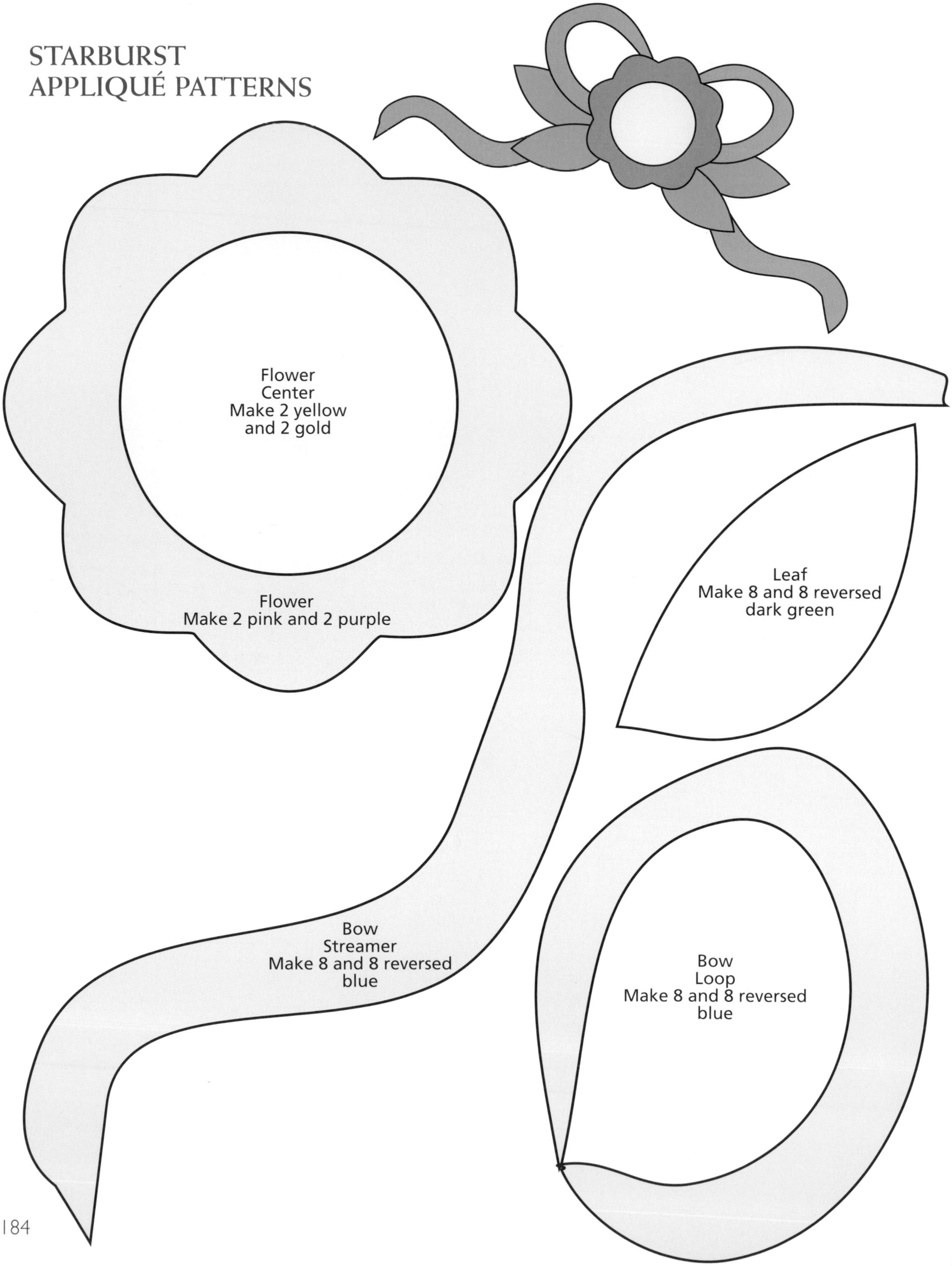

Flower
Center
Make 2 yellow
and 2 gold

Flower
Make 2 pink and 2 purple

Leaf
Make 8 and 8 reversed
dark green

Bow
Streamer
Make 8 and 8 reversed
blue

Bow
Loop
Make 8 and 8 reversed
blue

STARBURST
FOUNDATION PATTERN

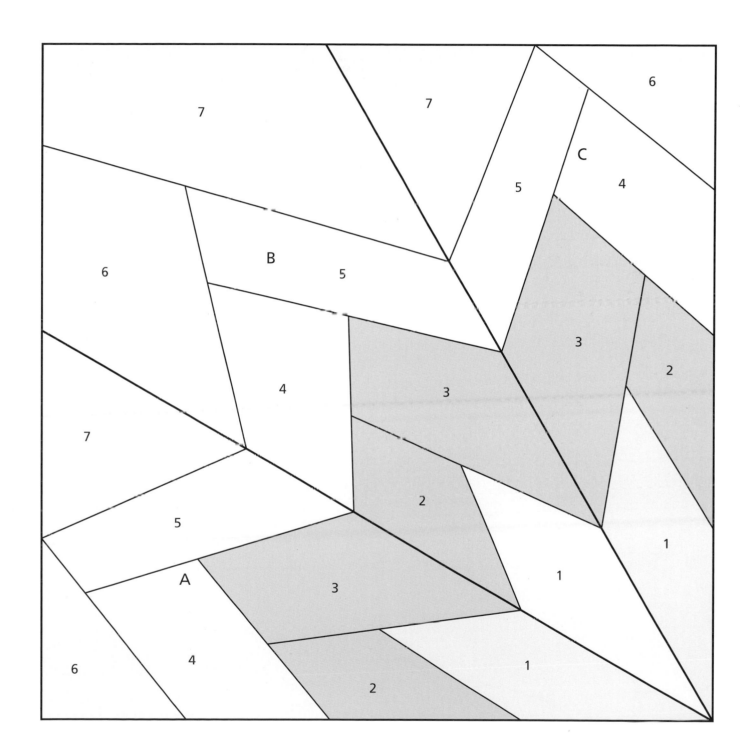

THE LIGHTHOUSE
APPLIQUÉ PATTERN—UPPER RIGHT

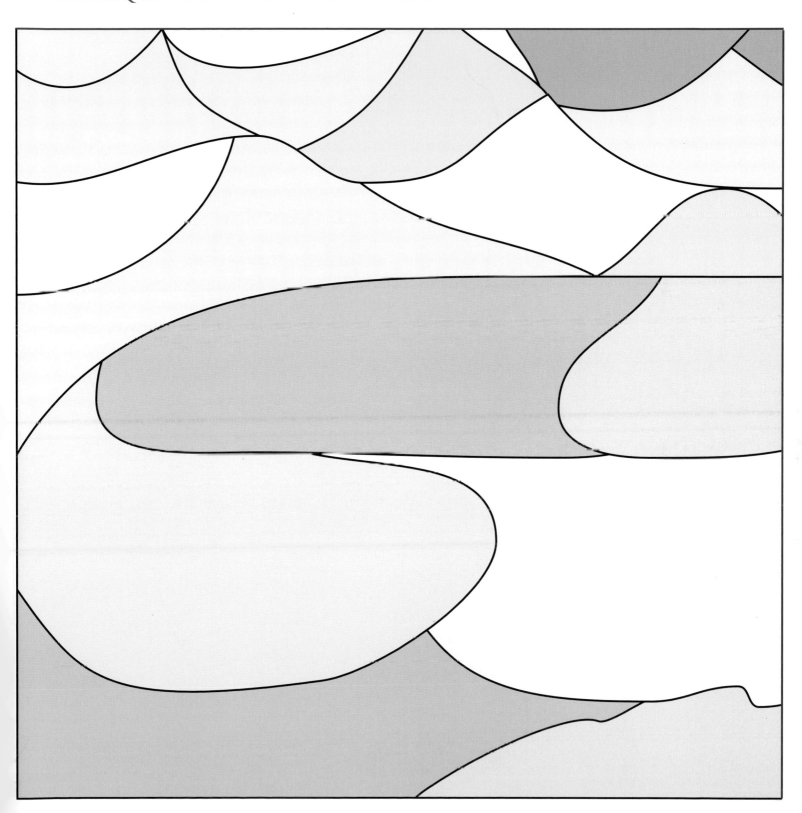

THE LIGHTHOUSE
APPLIQUÉ PATTERN—UPPER LEFT

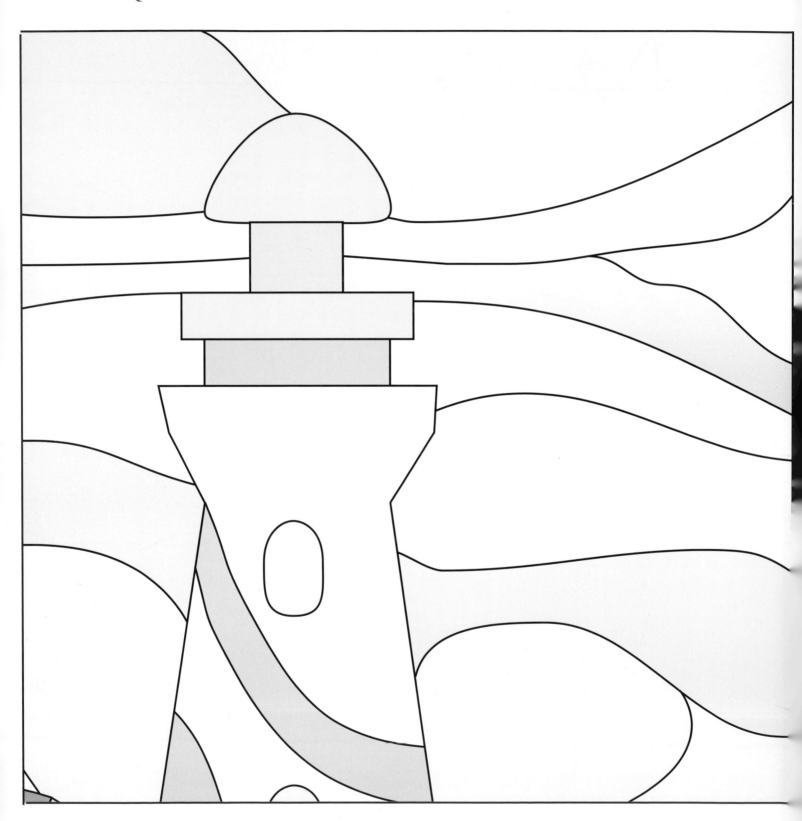

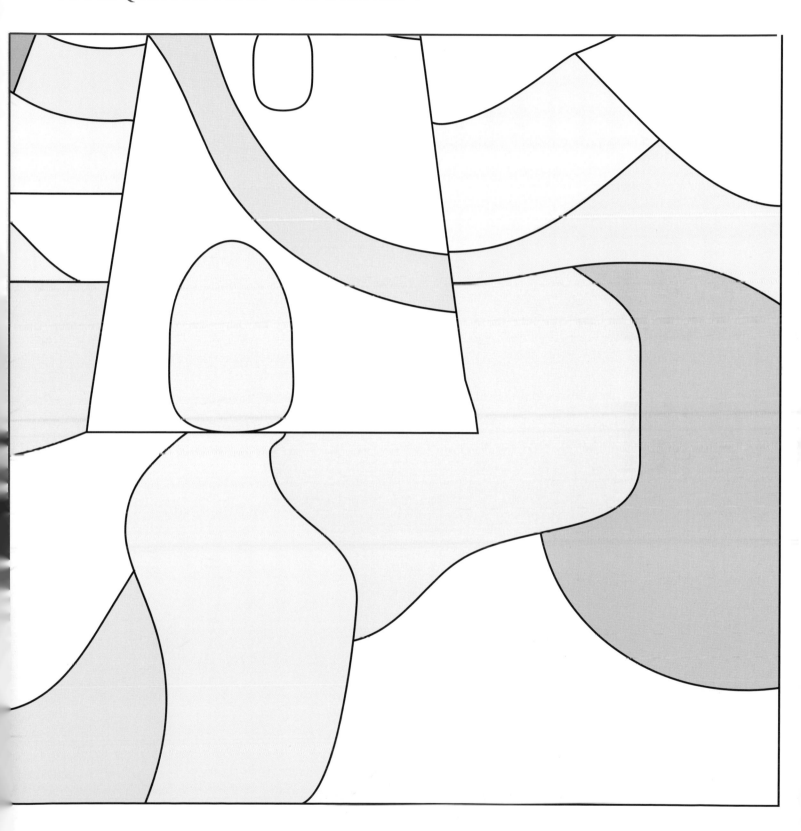

DRUNKARD'S PATH
TEMPLATES

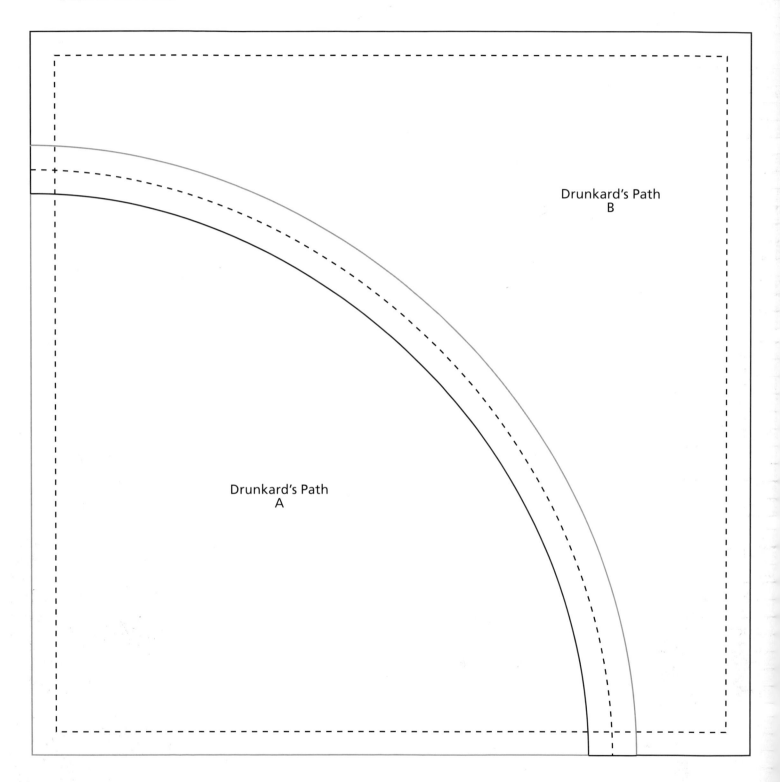

Drunkard's Path
B

Drunkard's Path
A

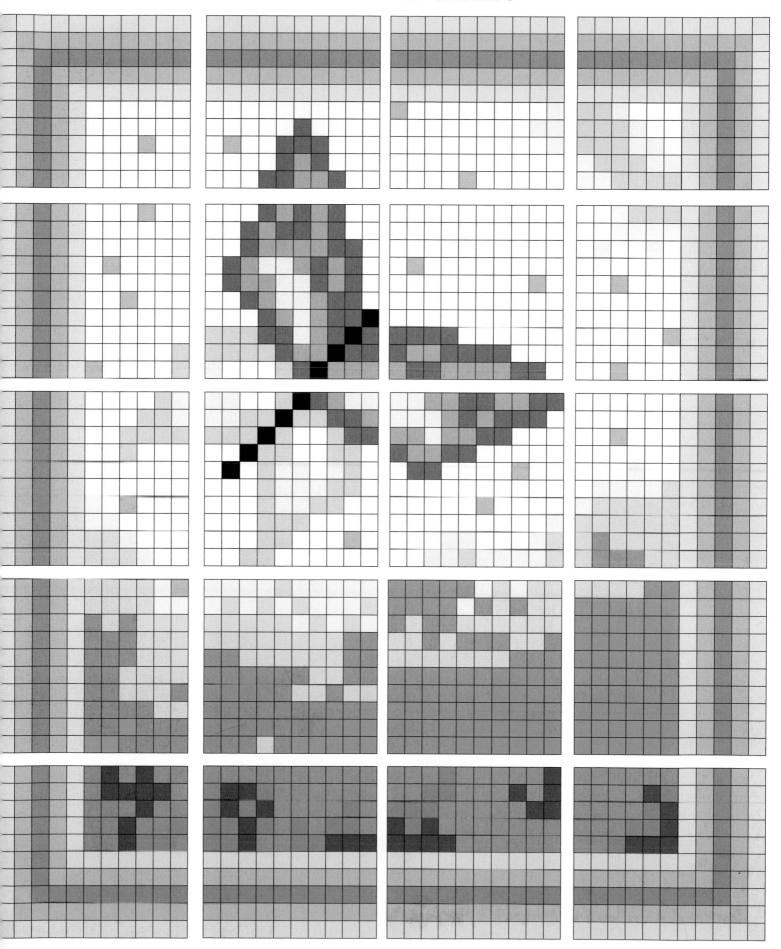

Index